Veloce *Classic Reprint* Series

Subaru
Impreza

Those Were The Days ... Series
Alpine Trials & Rallies 1910-1973 (Pfundner)
American 'Independent' Automakers – AMC to Willys 1945 to 1960 (Mort)
American Station Wagons – The Golden Era 1950-1975 (Mort)
American Trucks of the 1950s (Mort)
American Trucks of the 1960s (Mort)
American Woodies 1928-1953 (Mort)
Anglo-American Cars from the 1930s to the 1970s (Mort)
Austerity Motoring (Bobbitt)
Austins, The last real (Peck)
Brighton National Speed Trials (Gardiner)
British and European Trucks of the 1970s (Peck)
British Drag Racing – The early years (Pettitt)
British Lorries of the 1950s (Bobbitt)
British Lorries of the 1960s (Bobbitt)
British Touring Car Racing (Collins)
British Police Cars (Walker)
British Woodies (Peck)
Café Racer Phenomenon, The (Walker)
Don Hayter's MGB Story – The birth of the MGB in MG's Abingdon Design & Development Office (Hayter)
Drag Bike Racing in Britain – From the mid '60s to the mid '80s (Lee)
Dune Buggy Phenomenon, The (Hale)
Dune Buggy Phenomenon Volume 2, The (Hale)
Endurance Racing at Silverstone in the 1970s & 1980s (Parker)
Hot Rod & Stock Car Racing in Britain in the 1980s (Neil)
Mercedes-Benz Trucks (Peck)
MG's Abingdon Factory (Moylan)
Motor Racing at Brands Hatch in the Seventies (Parker)
Motor Racing at Brands Hatch in the Eighties (Parker)
Motor Racing at Crystal Palace (Collins)
Motor Racing at Goodwood in the Sixties (Gardiner)
Motor Racing at Nassau in the 1950s & 1960s (O'Neil)
Motor Racing at Oulton Park in the 1960s (McFadyen)
Motor Racing at Oulton Park in the 1970s (McFadyen)
Motor Racing at Thruxton in the 1970s (Grant-Braham)
Motor Racing at Thruxton in the 1980s (Grant-Braham)
Superprix – The Story of Birmingham Motor Race (Page & Collins)
Three Wheelers (Bobbitt)

Great Cars
Austin-Healey – A celebration of the fabulous 'Big' Healey (Piggott)
Jaguar E-type (Thorley)
Jaguar Mark 1 & 2 (Thorley)
Triumph TR – TR2 to 6: The last of the traditional sports cars (Piggott)

Rally Giants Series
Audi Quattro (Robson)
Austin Healey 100-6 & 3000 (Robson)
Fiat 131 Abarth (Robson)
Ford Escort MkI (Robson)
Ford Escort RS Cosworth & World Rally Car (Robson)
Ford Escort RS1800 (Robson)
Lancia Delta 4WD/Integrale (Robson)
Lancia Stratos (Robson)
Mini Cooper/Mini Cooper S (Robson)
Peugeot 205 T16 (Robson)
Saab 96 & V4 (Robson)
Subaru Impreza (Robson)
Toyota Celica GT4 (Robson)

WSC Giants
Audi R8 (Wagstaff)
Ferrari 312P & 312PB (Collins & McDonough)
Gulf-Mirage 1967 to 1982 (McDonough)
Matra Sports Cars – MS620, 630, 650, 660 & 670 – 1966 to 1974 (McDonough)

Biographies
A Chequered Life – Graham Warner and the Chequered Flag (Hesletine)
A Life Awheel – The 'auto' biography of W de Forte (Skelton)
Amédée Gordini ... a true racing legend (Smith)
André Lefebvre, and the cars he created at Voisin and Citroën (Beck)
Chris Carter at Large – Stories from a lifetime in motorcycle racing (Carter & Skelton)
Cliff Allison, The Official Biography of – From the Fells to Ferrari (Gauld)
Edward Turner – The Man Behind the Motorcycles (Clew)
Driven by Desire – The Desiré Wilson Story
First Principles – The Official Biography of Keith Duckworth (Burr)
Inspired to Design – F1 cars, Indycars & racing tyres: the autobiography of Nigel Bennett (Bennett)
Jack Sears, The Official Biography of – Gentleman Jack (Gauld)
Jim Redman – 6 Times World Motorcycle Champion: The Autobiography (Redman)
John Chatham – 'Mr Big Healey' – The Official Biography (Burr)
The Lee Noble Story (Wilkins)
Mason's Motoring Mayhem – Tony Mason's hectic life in motorsport and television (Mason)
Raymond Mays' Magnificent Obsession (Apps)
Pat Moss Carlsson Story, The – Harnessing Horsepower (Turner)
'Sox' – Gary Hocking – the forgotten World Motorcycle Champion (Hughes)
Tony Robinson – The biography of a race mechanic (Wagstaff)
Virgil Exner – Visioneer: The Official Biography of Virgil M Exner Designer Extraordinaire (Grist)

General
1½-litre GP Racing 1961-1965 (Whitelock)
AC Two-litre Saloons & Buckland Sportscars (Archibald)
Alpine & Renault – The Development of the Revolutionary Turbo F1 Car 1968 to 1979 (Smith)
Alpine & Renault – The Sports Prototypes 1963 to 1969 (Smith)
Alpine & Renault – The Sports Prototypes 1973 to 1978 (Smith)
An Austin Anthology (Stringer)
An Incredible Journey (Falls & Reisch)
Anatomy of the Classic Mini (Huthert & Ely)
Anatomy of the Works Minis (Moylan)
Austin Cars 1948 to 1990 – a pictorial history (Rowe)
Autodrome (Collins & Ireland)
Automotive A-Z, Lane's Dictionary of Automotive Terms (Lane)
Automotive Mascots (Kay & Springate)
Bahamas Speed Weeks, The (O'Neil)
Bluebird CN7 (Stevens)
BMC Competitions Department Secrets (Turner, Chambers & Browning)
British at Indianapolis, The (Wagstaff)
British Café Racers (Cloesen)
British Cars, The Complete Catalogue of, 1895-1975 (Culshaw & Horrobin)
British Custom Motorcycles – The Brit Chop – choppers, cruisers, bobbers & trikes (Cloesen)
BRM – A Mechanic's Tale (Salmon)
BRM V16 (Ludvigsen)
BSA Bantam Bible, The (Henshaw)
BSA Motorcycles – the final evolution (Jones)
Carrera Panamericana, La (Tipler)
Car-tastrophes – 80 automotive atrocities from the past 20 years (Honest John, Fowler)
Chrysler 300 – America's Most Powerful Car 2nd Edition (Ackerson)
Chrysler PT Cruiser (Ackerson)
Citroën DS (Bobbitt)
Classic British Car Electrical Systems (Astley)
Cobra – The Real Thing! (Legate)
Competition Car Aerodynamics 3rd Edition (McBeath)
Competition Car Composites A Practical Handbook (Revised 2nd Edition) (McBeath)
Concept Cars, How to illustrate and design – New 2nd Edition (Dewey)
Cortina – Ford's Bestseller (Robson)
Cosworth – The Search for Power (6th edition) (Robson)
Coventry Climax Racing Engines (Hammill)
Daily Mirror 1970 World Cup Rally 40, The (Robson)
Drive on the Wild Side, A – 20 Extreme Driving Adventures From Around the World (Weaver)
East German Motor Vehicles in Pictures (Suhr/Weinreich)
Essential Guide to Driving in Europe, The (Parish)
Fast Ladies – Female Racing Drivers 1888 to 1970 (Bouzanquet)
Fate of the Sleeping Beauties, The (op de Weegh/Hottendorff/op de Weegh)
Ferrari 288 GTO, The Book of the (Sackey)
Ferrari 333 SP (O'Neil)
Fiat & Abarth 124 Spider & Coupé (Tipler)
Fiat & Abarth 500 & 600 – 2nd Edition (Bobbitt)
Fiats, Great Small (Ward)
Ford Cleveland 335-Series V8 engine 1970 to 1982 – The Essential Source Book (Hammill)
Ford F100/F150 Pick-up 1948-1996 (Ackerson)
Ford F150 Pick-up 1997-2005 (Ackerson)
Ford Focus WRC (Robson)
Ford GT – Then, and Now (Streather)
Ford GT40 (Legate)
Ford Midsize Muscle – Fairlane, Torino & Ranchero (Cranswick)
Ford Model Y (Roberts)
Ford Small Block V8 Racing Engines 1962-1970 – The Essential Source Book (Hammill)
Formula One – The Real Score? (Harvey)
Formula 5000 Motor Racing, Back then ... and back now (Lawson)
Forza Minardi! (Vigar)
The Good, the Mad and the Ugly ... not to mention Jeremy Clarkson (Dron)
Grand Prix Ferrari – The Years of Enzo Ferrari's Power, 1948-1980 (Pritchard)
Grand Prix Ford – DFV-powered Formula 1 Cars (Robson)
GT – The World's Best GT Cars 1953-73 (Dawson)
Hillclimbing & Sprinting – The Essential Manual (Short & Wilkinson)
Honda NSX (Long)
Immortal Austin Seven (Morgan)
Karmann-Ghia Coupé & Convertible (Bobbitt)
Kawasaki Triples Bible, The (Walker)
Kris Meeke – Intercontinental Rally Challenge Champion (McBride)
Lancia 037 (Collins)
Lancia Delta HF Integrale (Blaettel & Wagner)
Lancia Delta Integrale (Collins)
Le Mans Panoramic (Ireland)
Lexus Story, The (Long)
Maserati 250F In Focus (Pritchard)
Maximum Mini (Booij)
Mercedes G-Wagen (Long)
MG, Made in Abingdon (Frampton)
MGA (Price Williams)
MGB & MGB GT– Expert Guide (Auto-doc Series) (Williams)
MGB Electrical Systems Updated & Revised Edition (Astley)
Micro Trucks (Mort)
Microcars at Large! (Quellin)
Mini Cooper – The Real Thing! (Tipler)
Mini Minor to Asia Minor (West)
Mitsubishi Lancer Evo, The Road Car & WRC Story (Long)
Montlhéry, The Story of the Paris Autodrome (Boddy)
MOPAR Muscle – Barracuda, Dart & Valiant 1960-1980 (Cranswick)
Morgan Maverick (Lawrence)
Morgan 3 Wheeler – back to the future!, The (Dron)
Morris Minor, 70 Years on the Road (Newell)
Motor Racing – Reflections of a Lost Era (Carter)
Motor Racing – The Pursuit of Victory 1930-1962 (Carter)
Motor Racing – The Pursuit of Victory 1963-1972 (Wyatt/Sears)
Motor Racing Heroes – The Stories of 100 Greats (Newman)
Motorcycle Apprentice (Cakebread)
Motorcycle GP Racing in the 1960s (Pereira)
Motorcycle Racing with the Continental Circus 1920-1970 (Pereira)
Motorcycle Road & Racing Chassis Designs (Noakes)
Motorcycling in the '50s (Clew)
Motorhomes, The Illustrated History (Jenkinson)
Motorsport In colour, 1950s (Wainwright)
MV Agusta Fours, The book of the classic (Falloon)
N.A.R.T. – A concise history of the North American Racing Team 1957 to 1983 (O'Neil)
Nissan 300ZX & 350Z – The Z-Car Story (Long)
Nissan GT-R Supercar: Born to race (Gorodji)
Northeast American Sports Car Races 1950-1959 (O'Neil)
Norton Commando Bible – All models 1968 to 1978 (Henshaw)
Nothing Runs – Misadventures in the Classic, Collectable & Exotic Car Biz (Slutsky)
Off-Road Giants! (Volume 1) – Heroes of 1960s Motorcycle Sport (Westlake)
Off-Road Giants! (Volume 2) – Heroes of 1960s Motorcycle Sport (Westlake)
Off-Road Giants! (Volume 3) – Heroes of 1960s Motorcycle Sport (Westlake)
Pass the Theory and Practical Driving Tests (Gibson & Hoole)
Peking to Paris 2007 (Young)
Pontiac Firebird – New 3rd Edition (Cranswick)
Preston Tucker & Others (Linde)
RAC Rally Action! (Gardiner)
Racing Colours – Motor Racing Compositions 1908-2009 (Newman)
Racing Line – British motorcycle racing in the golden age of the big single (Guntrip)
Rallye Sport Fords: The Inside Story (Moreton)
The Red Baron's Ultimate Ducati Desmo Manual (Cabrera Choclán)
Renewable Energy Home Handbook, The (Porter)
Roads with a View – England's greatest views and how to find them by road (Corfield)
Rolls-Royce Silver Shadow/Bentley T Series Corniche & Camargue – Revised & Enlarged Edition (Bobbitt)
Rolls-Royce Silver Spirit, Silver Spur & Bentley Mulsanne 2nd Edition (Bobbitt)
Rootes Cars of the 50s, 60s & 70s – Hillman, Humber, Singer, Sunbeam & Talbot (Rowe)
Rover P4 (Bobbitt)
Runways & Racers (O'Neil)
Russian Motor Vehicles – Soviet Limousines 1930-2003 (Kelly)
Russian Motor Vehicles – The Czarist Period 1784 to 1917 (Kelly)
RX-7 – Mazda's Rotary Engine Sportscar (Updated & Revised New Edition) (Long)
Scooters & Microcars, The A-Z of Popular (Dan)
Scooter Lifestyle (Grainger)
Scooter Mania! – Recollections of the Isle of Man International Scooter Rally (Jackson)
Singer Story: Cars, Commercial Vehicles, Bicycles & Motorcycle (Atkinson)
Sleeping Beauties USA – abandoned classic cars & trucks (Marek)
SM – Citroën's Maserati-engined Supercar (Long & Claverol)
Speedway – Auto racing's ghost tracks (Collins & Ireland)
Sprite Caravans, The Story of (Jenkinson)
Standard Motor Company, The Book of the (Robson)
Steve Hole's Kit Car Cornucopia – Cars, Companies, Stories, Facts & Figures: the UK's kit car scene since 1949 (Hole)
Subaru Impreza: The Road Car And WRC Story (Long)
Supercar, How to Build your own (Thompson)
Tales from the Toolbox (Oliver)
Tatra – The Legacy of Hans Ledwinka, Updated & Enlarged Collector's Edition of 1500 copies (Margolius & Henry)
Taxi! The Story of the 'London' Taxicab (Bobbitt)
This Day in Automotive History (Corey)
To Boldly Go – twenty six vehicle designs that dared to be different (Hull)
Toleman Story, The (Hilton)
Toyota Celica & Supra, The Book of Toyota's Sports Coupés (Long)
Toyota MR2 Coupés & Spyders (Long)
Triumph & Standard Cars 1945 to 1984 (Warrington)
Triumph Bonneville Bible (59-83) (Henshaw)
Triumph Bonneville!, Save the – The inside story of the Meriden Workers' Co-op (Rosamond)
Triumph Motorcycles & the Meriden Factory (Hancox)
Triumph Speed Twin & Thunderbird Bible (Woolridge)
Triumph Tiger Cub Bible (Estall)
Triumph Trophy Bible (Woolridge)
Triumph TR6 (Kimberley)
TT Talking – The TT's most exciting era – As seen by Manx Radio TT's lead commentator 2004-2012 (Lambert)
Two Summers – The Mercedes-Benz W196R Racing Car (Ackerson)
TWR Story, The – Group A (Hughes & Scott)
Unraced (Collins)
Velocette Motorcycles – MSS to Thruxton – Third Edition (Burris)
Vespa – The Story of a Cult Classic in Pictures (Uhlig)
Vincent Motorcycles: The Untold Story since 1946 (Guyony & Parker)
Volkswagen Bus Book, The (Bobbitt)
Volkswagen Bus or Van to Camper, How to Convert (Porter)
Volkswagens of the World (Glen)
VW Beetle Cabriolet – The full story of the convertible Beetle (Bobbitt)
VW Beetle – The Car of the 20th Century (Copping)
VW Bus – 40 Years of Splitties, Bays & Wedges (Copping)
VW Bus Book, The (Bobbitt)
VW Golf: Five Generations of Fun (Copping & Cservenka)
VW – The Air-cooled Era (Copping)
VW T5 Camper Conversion Manual (Porter)
VW Campers (Copping)
Volkswagen Type 3, The book of the – Concept, Design, International Production Models & Development (Glen)
Volvo Estate, The (Hollebone)
You & Your Jaguar XK8/XKR – Buying, Enjoying, Maintaining, Modifying – New Edition (Thorley)
Which Oil? – Choosing the right oils & greases for your antique, vintage, veteran, classic or collector car (Michell)
Wolseley Cars 1948 to 1975 (Rowe)
Works Minis, The Last (Purves & Brenchley)
Works Rally Mechanic (Moylan)

www.veloce.co.uk

Also available ... Apps Download now from www.digital.veloce.co.uk

Hubble & Hattie

Belvedere

Also available ... eBook Download now from www.digital.veloce.co.uk

First published under ISBN 978-1-84584-042-9 in November 2006 by Veloce Publishing Limited, Veloce House, Parkway Farm Business Park, Middle Farm Way, Poundbury, Dorchester DT1 3AR, England. Fax 01305 268864/Tel 01305 260068/e-mail info@veloce.co.uk/web www.veloce.co.uk or www.velocebooks.com
Veloce Classic Reprint edition published April 2018.
ISBN: 978-1-787113-22-0. UPC: 6-36847-01322-6
© Graham Robson and Veloce Publishing 2006 & 2018. All rights reserved. With the exception of quoting brief passages for the purpose of review, no part of this publication may be recorded, reproduced or transmitted by any means, including photocopying, without the written permission of Veloce Publishing Ltd. Throughout this book logos, model names and designations, etc, have been used for the purposes of identification, illustration and decoration. Such names are the property of the trademark holder as this is not an official publication.
Readers with ideas for automotive books, or books on other transport or related hobby subjects, are invited to write to the editorial director of Veloce Publishing at the above address.
British Library Cataloguing in Publication Data - A catalogue record for this book is available from the British Library. Typesetting, design and page make-up all by Veloce Publishing Ltd on Apple Mac.
Printed and bound by CPI Group (UK) Ltd, Croydon, CR0 4YY.

Veloce *Classic Reprint* Series

RALLY GIANTS™

Subaru
Impreza

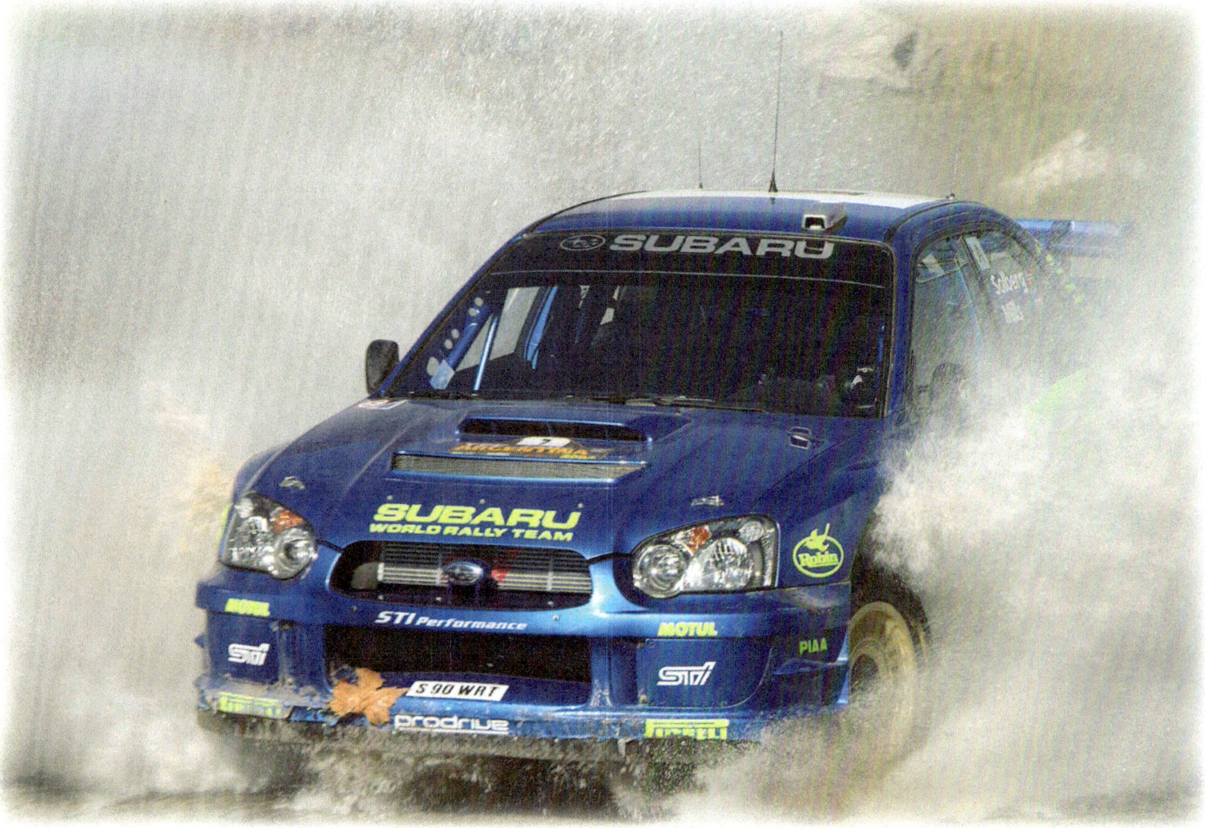

Graham Robson

Contents

Foreword .. 5
Introduction .. 7
Acknowledegments .. 8
The car and the team .. 9
    Inspiration .. 9
    The Impreza's importance in rallying .. 11
    Facing up to rival cars .. 13
    Homologation – meeting the rules .. 15
    Engineering features .. 16
    Impreza World Rally Car .. 26
    Was the Impreza unique? .. 37
    Building and running the works cars .. 37
    Personalities and star drivers .. 38
Competition story .. 52
    The Impreza's career .. 52
    1993 .. 52
    1994 .. 54
    1995 .. 59
    1996 .. 66
    1997 .. 74
    1998 .. 81
    1999 .. 86
    2000 .. 91
    2001 .. 93
    2002 .. 97
    2003 .. 103
    2004 .. 106
    2005 .. 110
    The Impreza's successor .. 116
Works rally cars – World Championship rallies (and when first used) .. 118
World/major European rally wins .. 121
Index .. 123

Toyota, Mazda, Mitsubishi and Subaru, though the Mazda was under-powered and the Subaru Legacy too new to figure.

Although Ford had re-emerged as a real challenger in 1993, the biggest innovation was the arrival of a new car from Subaru – the Impreza – which swept away every single failing of the old Legacy. By then, no question, a sport which had been dominated by European makers was now to be dominated by cars from Japan.

The Japanese, however, had not merely invested huge amounts of money in this programme, but had hired in the best European brains and businesses to do the job for them. Is it fair to suggest that Japanese rally cars prepared in Japan still lacked a world perspective, and that they needed European expertise to rectify this?

Subaru, in fact, made its big decision and spread out a new strategy: to its credit, Subaru then stuck to it through thick and thin. By the end of 2005, the Impreza had already completed thirteen years at World level, Within a year of its launch it became a winner, and ten years later it was still winning against the very toughest competition. Car shapes, styling alterations, aerodynamics, equipment details and almost every mechanical detail may have changed over that time, but the same basic motor car – the same platform, flat-4 engine and four-wheel drive transmission – linked every single derivative. Every car was blue, with yellow

Subaru and four-wheel drive

Although four-wheel drive machines have been with us for at least one hundred years, it was not until the 1960s that the first four-wheel drive private cars (as opposed to commercial and military vehicles) went on sale. Jensen, with the FF of 1966, provided the first such European machine, but it was not until 1974 that Subaru introduced four-wheel drive versions of its Leone models, which usually had only front-wheel drive.

Jeeps and Land Rovers had four-wheel drive because they needed ultimate traction on all surfaces, while Jensen provided it only to spread immense power to four-wheels, to give ultimate balance and roadholding. Subaru's Leone models, with 1.1-litre or 1.4-litre engines, certainly did not produce huge amounts of power, but the light commercial derivatives of this type provided a USP (unique selling proposition) compared with their rivals.

Initial systems were cheap-and-cheerful, but undeniably effective, and by the 1980s Subaru found that its image was growing strongly on the back of this feature. Small-engined Subaru city cars did not have this feature, but as four-wheel drive (optional in many cases, but sometimes standard, depending on the model) was introduced on larger and more expensive models, the USP of Subaru + 4WD + grip-and-security became entrenched.

Even so, although two of Subaru's Japanese rivals – Mitsubishi and Toyota – made haste to introduce four-wheel drive machinery in the mid-1980s, this was only done so that those companies could have a competitive machine with which to go rallying.

Accordingly, when an even larger and more ambitious Subaru, the Legacy, first appeared in 1989, its 'entry level' model had front-wheel drive, but a new and more advanced four-wheel drive installation was an integral part of the mid-range and upper-range models.

Since that time, four-wheel drive has become more and more prominent in the Subaru line-up. In 2005/06 four-wheel drive figured in every Subaru production car, from the 0.7-litre R1 mini-car, through the Justy, the Impreza and Legacy private cars, and was naturally ever-present in the SUVs and 'cross-over' models which topped out the range.

Championship. Even so, engine reliability was still a problem, and it was clear that the Legacy was not an ideal tarmac car.

By 1992 the Legacy was as competitive as it was ever likely to be. With the new Escort RS Cosworth in the wings, and with Toyota's latest Celica at its peak, there would perhaps never be another chance for fame. Unhappily, though, the Legacy still struggled to be competitive.

Although there were several good finishes – second in the Swedish (Colin McRae), fourth in Greece (McRae), fourth in the 1000 Lakes (Ari Vatanen), and second in the RAC (Vatanen), Colin McRae still indulged in expensive accidents, engines continued to let go, and the Prodrive team rarely looked like winning events. In Britain, however, there was consolation, where Colin McRae won all six rounds of the British Rally Championship.

By this time, in any case, Subaru and Prodrive had both realised that if they were to start winning, they needed a new and more compact car than before. The inspiration – and it was certainly a direct comparison with what was to follow – was what Ford's works team was already doing to get back into a winning position once again.

Here was a perfect example: the original Sierra RS Cosworth had been a great race car, but lacked the four-wheel drive which would have made it ideal for rallying. The Sierra Cosworth 4x4 got its four-wheel drive, but was not only too heavy, but distressingly unreliable in its first two seasons. Sheer hard work had then turned this car into a reliable podium finisher but not a winner. This led Ford's own works team (not the mainstream engineers) to create the Escort RS Cosworth; a smaller, lighter and altogether more nimble car than the Sierra, but one which used the same now-proven engine and drive line. Refined while the Legacy was making its name, the latest Escort soon showed that the theory was about to match the practice: well before Subaru could possibly react, it had gone on sale, been homologated, and had started winning.

Subaru's response, influenced (but by no means driven) by Ford, was to carry out a similar exercise. Advised at every stage by Prodrive, it concentrated future efforts on the still-secret four-wheel drive Impreza. Smaller, lighter, more manoeuvrable and – guess what? – powered by the same basic flat-4 power unit, transmission and running gear, it showed every promise of doing the job. Well before the new car was even launched, Subaru had mocked up – and tested – short-wheelbase Legacy types to prove its point, and by the time the cars went on sale, rallying activity was imminent.

The Impreza's importance in rallying

The launch of the Impreza confirmed that the Japanese motor industry was serious about achieving dominance in World rallying, not that this was ever going to be easy. Although Honda had taken very little time to produce the most powerful race engines in Formula 1, car manufacturers had already discovered that the rough-and-tumble, ever-changing world of rallying set altogether more complicated problems.

Deep thinkers in Europe, however, were already worried about the consistent improvement among the Japanese teams. Because Toyota was already a rally winner (Carlos Sainz, after all, had won the 1990 and 1992 World Championships in four-wheel drive Celicas, though Toyota had not yet won the Makes series), the media and rally enthusiasts were already accustomed to Japanese cars taking many victories.

Stuart Turner, recently retired from his high-profile position in Ford Motorsport, was still ever-present on the motorsport chat show circuit, and often had to field the same question: "What is your advice for young drivers trying to break into top-level motorsport?" Without hesitation, his reply was: "Learn to speak Japanese!" Maybe there was an element of levity in that response, but the intention was clear.

The imminent arrival of the Impreza WRX, or Turbo (it was to be given different titles in different markets), therefore emphasised the change that had occurred in World rallying. In the mid-1980s, for instance, Lancia, Peugeot and Audi had been dominant, without a Japanese manufacturer even in the frame. By 1990, Lancia was strongly challenged by

Japanese cars in rallying

Because rallying was initially a European-only sport, the Japanese motor industry was not interested in taking part at first. It was only when European-style rallies spread to countries dominated by ex-pats (in Africa and Australasia, for instance) that Japanese importers in those countries decided to get involved.

First in Australia, then in East Africa (where the Safari garnered huge amounts of publicity), it was Nissan-Datsun that first put up works sponsored teams. Rugged saloons were then backed up by 240Z Coupés, and these cars were mainly prepared in the UK, though Nissan then went on to prepare cars in Japan in the 1970s and 1980s. Their major successes included several outright victories in the East African Safari. Nissan produced an unsuccessful Sunny/Pulsar GTi-R Group B car in the 1980s, and, thereafter, withdrew from the sport.

Like Nissan-Datsun, Mitsubishi first took an interest in rallies in the 1970s, when its Colt Lancer won the Safari. Successes then followed in Australian events, but the big breakthrough came in 1988 when the turbocharged four-wheel drive Galant VR-4 appeared. Bolstered up by a UK-based programme, and with competitive European drivers hired, Mitsubishi then produced the Lancer RS with which Tommi Makinen would win won four consecutive World Drivers' Championships (1996-99 inclusive).

Employing the famous Swedish rally driver, Ove Andersson, first as a driver, then as a consultant who opened a tuning house (TTE) in Germany, Toyota started modestly, but won several African endurance events with Celica Twin-Cam Turbo coupés in the 1980s. The Celica GT-Four then appeared in 1988, and Carlos Sainz turned it into a regular winner from 1989, after which Toyota became an enduring power on the rally scene. Shame and ignominy then followed at the end of 1995, when the company was caught out over blatant flouting of engine technical regulations, and was banned for a period. By the end of the 1990s Toyota had turned its back on rallying, in favour of a heavily-financed assault on F1.

It was against this domestic background that Subaru was encouraged to take an interest in rallying, where it would soon become competitive and – by 1995 – the standard-setter for all other world-class car manufacturers.

Subaru and Prodrive agreed that while Subaru would provide most of the Group A hardware, Prodrive would control the development effort, run the cars, and hire the drivers. Subaru was due to launch the Legacy in Europe towards the end of 1989, so it was agreed that the works cars could be put on the start-line of major events in 1990. Because the Japanese were totally serious in their intent, it was always agreed that, because time was short, the Prodrive cars would have to be based on the four-wheel drive Legacy RS, rather than any limited-production 'homologation special' that could have been evolved from it.

Thus it was that the toe-in-the-water operation became a major rally programme for, year-on-year, the Legacy became more and more impressive. First homologated on 1 January 1990, the first STI entry was in the Safari where one car took sixth, but four others suffered overheating engines. The first STI-Europe (Prodrive) Legacy started the Acropolis in June (the suspension wilted and the engine blew), 'Possum' Bourne's STI car was fifth in New Zealand and fourth in Australia, while Markku Alen's Prodrive car took fourth in the 1000 Lakes.

Things then got better, and the cars became somewhat more reliable, in 1991. Not only did Subaru RT Europe (Prodrive) driver Markku Alen rack up third in Sweden, fourth in New Zealand and Australia, but Colin McRae took four outright wins in the UK to win the British Rally

The car and the team

Inspiration

By the end of the 1980s, Subaru had noted how two of its Japanese rivals – Toyota and Mitsubishi – were gaining so much good publicity from the use of their four-wheel drive Celicas and Galants in rallying. Although Subaru would not lose 'face' by keeping away ('face' being important in Japanese business), it concluded that there was much to be gained from a successful World rally programme.

Although works Subarus had already been seen in rallying (the first important foray was in the 1980 Safari), this was mainly with under-powered but solidly-prepared cars in the Safari, Australasia, and other events in Asia. Even so, up to the end of the 1980s it had made no serious, concentrated attempt to break into European rallying or (apart from the Safari) into major World events.

The template was already clear – to beat its domestic rivals and the Lancia Integrale, it would need a nimble turbocharged four-wheel drive car which could develop at least 300bhp. And there was the problem: even after a great deal of development, Subaru had not yet put such a car in production which could be expected to win.

Even so, the masterplan was already in place. In April 1988, a new subsidiary, STI (Subaru Tecnica International), was founded to manage, promote and engineer Subaru's motorsports activities. In January 1989, the new range of Legacy saloons and estate cars made their debut. At the peak of this range was the Legacy RS model, which combined a 16-valve turbocharged 220bhp/1994cc flat-4 engine, with four-wheel drive, all tucked into a body of similar dimensions (and weight) to Ford's Sierra Cosworth. This, surely, would be a good basis on which to go rallying.

STI laid down a marker early on when it sent out a Legacy RS to a high-speed test track in Arizona, USA, where it set a new FIA endurance speed record, of 62,150 miles/100,000km at no less than 138.80mph/223.345km/h.

Although Subaru had been wedded to flat-4 engines for some years, this new 'boxer' was brand new, and was linked to a re-worked four-wheel drive system, complete with a viscous coupling centre differential. All-independent suspension was by MacPherson strut at front and rear, this being coupled to power-assisted rack-and-pinion steering, and allied to four-wheel disc brakes. However, because this was no homologation special, it was quite a heavy car (the RS was quoted at 2844lb/1290kg), and no less than 14ft 9.5in long.

It was all very promising, though Subaru realised that the company was not likely to make that major breakthrough unless it tapped into a mountain of existing expertise, which meant hiring a European-based organisation to do the job. STI (Subaru Technica International) would continue to supply cars from Japan for Asian/Australasian/Safari events, whereas a new team, STI Europe, would get involved in the balance of the World operation.

Wisely, Subaru took time to make a choice, but eventually did the deal with David Richards' Banbury-based Prodrive concern. One major factor in that decision was that 'DR' (as he is often known) had impeccable connections with British American Tobacco, which meant that he was eventually (but not at first) able to persuade that organisation to provide major sponsorship for a rally programme: both Rothmans and 555 were cigarette brands owned by the BAT colossus, its worldwide promotional and advertising spend being prodigious. 555 was particularly strongly promoted in the Far East.

to a four-door style from 2001. Along the way there were annual changes, especially around the nose, where the rally cars always followed suit with the production machinery, and where there was a constant battle to improve the aerodynamics and the flow of cool air into, through, and out of the engine bay. Detail-lovers will compare one year's Impreza with another, and see the way that things were gradually changing.

If there was any feature which pundits were justified in criticising, it was Subaru and Prodrive's unflinching loyalty to Pirelli tyres. In modern times, teams like Ford seemed to swap allegiance at regular intervals – Michelin and Pirelli both figured on the Focus WRCs, for instance – to take advantage of new technology and marketing realities: Prodrive, though, always used Pirelli through thick and thin – and this was not always wise, for there were times when the team had to grudgingly admit that the tyres were struggling. In Subaru and Prodrive's lives, though, loyalty and long-term commitment meant more than grasping a momentary edge.

Like all the modern-generation teams, Subaru and Pirelli have had to deal with an ever-expanding programme. Companies like Ford, Lancia and Audi never had to deal with 16-event World Rally Championships, with events being held on every continent. Although the events themselves became shorter – rallysprints rather than 'real' rallies, the traditionalists might complain – this was still a gruelling way to go about motorsport.

To cope with this, not only did the team get larger, and even better resourced, but many more individual rally cars had to be involved. Fans of other makes could sometimes home in on one particular car, giving it pet names for its registration plate or its colour schemes, but this never happened with an Impreza.

Even so, when I came to 'do the math', I was astonished to realise that by the 2000s I could identify up to 20 new works cars being built every year, and that getting on for 150 individual machines had taken shape by the mid-2000s. To which you have to add survey cars, show cars, replicas for private owners, cars for drivers in other countries …

In the mid-1990s, the use of a handful of British American Tobacco 'publicity' registration numbers – which changed cars the way that you and I change shirts – had disguised the real facts about the number of cars being used. One only has to look at the preparation facilities enjoyed by Prodrive (they are close to the M40 at Banbury, and easy to see) to realise that this was always a sizeable operation.

One day, of course, the Impreza's career in World rallying will end, but by that time I am sure it will have won more events than any other of its rivals. By any standards that makes it a real Rally Giant.

Acknowledgements

In assembling all the facts, figures and illustrations for this book, I want to thank two individuals for making my job so much easier …

Every year, Martin Holmes Rallying produces a magnificent survey of the season's rallies, not only at World, but at many other levels too. The first such annual – *World Rallying 1* – covered the 1978 season, and at the time of writing a continuous run of 28 such volumes has made a study of rallying, rally cars and individuals both absorbing and enjoyable.

Many of the facts and statistics which appear in these pages have been checked and double-checked against *World Rallying*, making a difficult job that much easier.

Assembling the illustrations for this book was made much easier by the untiring efforts of my fellow author, Brian Long. Not only has Brian already produced a definitive study of Impreza road cars, he also lives in Japan and has access to the Subaru factory and the very helpful staff who guided him towards all the colour illustrations you see here.

Graham Robson

Introduction & acknowledgements

Introduction

This is really the story of two enterprises, and several cars, and I hope that what follows gives a flavour of what it was all about. Not only is this a book about a rally car – the turbocharged Impreza – but about Prodrive, which has run the works competition cars since the very beginning.

Subaru of Japan not only set up the STI division to develop high-performance versions of its cars, but over the years has been consistent in supporting the way that the four-wheel drive turbocharged Imprezas have become world-beating rally cars.

For nearly twenty years, Prodrive of Banbury, England, has provided the expertise, and the know-how, to help turn Subaru's vision into success. I have always admired the ultra-professional, single-minded, and ultimately successful way in which Prodrive has gone about its business, and the ongoing Impreza rally programme has been a classic example of its work. It was for all those reasons that I chose to look at the Impreza family as a Rally Giant – a car, a commitment, and a rally programme which was always intended to reflect what the Subaru company was all about.

Once Subaru decided to get involved in World Championship rallying, there was never any lack of ongoing interest on its part. Certainly it did not just design and develop the original car, before casting it out into the wide world to let it find its own level. Even so, when Subaru set out on this quest in 1989, can it have had any idea that the same basic mechanical layout – a low-mounted turbocharged flat-4 engine up front, and permanent four-wheel drive – would still be in use, still be being evolved, and still be competitive into the second half of the 2000s?

Like other cars also covered in this Rally Giants series, the Impreza soon became a real icon among enthusiasts. It wasn't just that it was fast, but that it made all the right noises. It wasn't just that a works Impreza was always so recognisable (that overall blue, with yellow livery has been consistent throughout, and every works car used Pirelli tyres), but that the personalities in the project were so famous, and successful, on their own account.

Although it was Subaru's resolve, and finance, which made this programme possible, it was David Richards' vision which made it certain that Prodrive would do a supreme job in running the team. 300+ bhp was one thing, but it needed a series of real rally driver legends – Ari Vatanen, Colin McRae, Carlos Sainz, Richard Burns and Petter Solberg among them – to bring the beasts to glorious and charismatic life.

More than some of the other Rally Giants that I intend to cover, the Impreza started life as it was always meant to be, rather than as a blank canvas on which some engineering genius could paint his technical pictures. Whereas a Ford Escort needed a different gearbox, rear transmission and rear suspension to become competitive, all such things had been considered on the Impreza at the concept stage. Even before cars were built, studies of internal and external air flow had already taken place.

For the Impreza, though, much of my praise is reserved for those managers and visionaries who could make sure that the cars improved from season to season. In concept, for sure, a 2005 Impreza WRC was the same as the original Impreza Turbo of 1993, but almost every component had been changed in the interim period.

The original rally car, after all, was a four-door saloon, but became a two-door WRC from 1997, then reverted the Austin-Healey 3000, and the latest is any one of the ten-off World Rally Cars which we see on our TV screens or on the special stages of the world.

Although rally regulations changed persistently over the years, the two most important events were four-wheel drive being authorised from 1980, and the 'World Rally Car' formula (which required only 20 identical cars to be produced to gain homologation) being adopted in 1997. At all times, however, successful rally cars have needed to blend high performance with strength and reliability. Unlike Grand Prix cars, they have needed to be built so that major repairs could be carried out at the side of the road, in the dark, sometimes in freezing cold, and sometimes in blazing temperatures.

Over the years, some cars became dominant, only to be eclipsed when new and more advanced rivals appeared. New cars appeared almost every year, but dramatically better machines appeared less often. From time to time rally enthusiasts would be astonished by a new model, and it was on occasions like that when a new rallying landmark was set.

So, which were the most important new cars to appear in the last half century? What is it that made them special at the time? In some cases it was perfectly obvious – Lancia's Stratos was the first-ever purpose-built rally car, the Audi Quattro was the first rally-winning four-wheel drive car, and the Toyota Celica GT4 was the first rally-winning four-wheel drive Group A car to come from Japan.

But what about Ford's original Escort? Or the Fiat 131 Abarth? Or the Lancia Delta Integrale? Or, of course, the Subaru Impreza? All of them had something unique to offer at the time, in comparison with their competitors. Because they offered something different, and raised rallying's standards even further, they were true Rally Giants.

To a rallying petrol-head like me, it would have been easy to choose twenty, thirty or even more rally cars that have made a difference to the sport. However, I have had to be brutal and cull my list to the very minimum. Listed here, in chronological order, are the 'Giant' cars I have picked out, to tell the ongoing story of world-class rallying in the last fifty years:

Car	Period used as a works car
Austin-Healey 3000	1959-1965
Saab 96 and V4	1960-1976
Mini Cooper/Cooper S	1962-1970
Ford Escort MkI	1968-1975
Lancia Stratos	1974-1981
Ford Escort MkII	1975-1981
Fiat 131 Abarth	1976-1981
Audi Quattro and S1	1981-1986
Peugeot 205T16	1984-1986
Lancia Delta 4x4/Integrale	1987-1993
Toyota Celica GT4	1988-1995
Ford Escort RS Cosworth/WRC	1993-1998
Subaru Impreza Turbo/WRC	1993-2006

There is so much to know, to tell, and to enjoy about each of these cars that I plan to devote a compact book to each one. And to make sure that one can be compared with another, I intend to keep the same format to each volume.

Graham Robson

Foreword

What is a rally? Today's events, for sure, are completely different from those of a hundred or even fifty years ago. What was once a test of reliability is now a test of speed and strength. What was once a long-distance trial is now a series of short-distance races.

In the beginning, rallying was all about using standard cars in long-distance road events, but by the 1950s the events were toughening up. Routes became rougher, target speeds were raised, point-to-point speed tests on special stages were introduced, and high-performance machines were needed to ensure victory.

Starting in the late 1950s, too, teams began developing extra-special versions of standard cars, these were built in small numbers and were meant only to go rallying or motor racing. These were the 'homologation specials' that now dominate the sport. The first of these, unquestionably, was

When the time came to introduce the Prodrive Imprezas into World rallying, the team ran a well-oiled, very detailed service and support operation. This was Finland in 1993.

livery (sometimes with 555 sponsorship, sometimes not), and every car would run on Pirelli tyres. Of how many other rally cars could consistency like that be quoted?

Facing up to rival cars

By 1992, when rally development of the new Impreza Turbo got under way, World rallying had settled down to a five-way battle between five determined manufacturers – Lancia, Toyota, Ford, Mitsubishi and Subaru – three of the five being Japanese. Nissan's attempt to join the 'top table' had failed due to some fundamental faults in the layout of its specially-developed car.

Because of the way that Group A rally regulations were applied, each of the competitive manufacturers was using a turbocharged 2-litre engine, all had well over 300bhp, and in most conditions they could all get down close to

In 1993, the original four-wheel-drive Impreza road car looked impressive, even before rally development and rally livery were applied.

first year, 1993, and the Escort World Rally Car of 1997-98 would be an incremental improvement.

Lancia Delta Integrale – front transverse-engine, four-wheel drive. The established long-term favourite, with a success record stretching back to 1987, when it was the less-powerful Delta HF 4x4. A multiple world champion in the Makes series, and for the lucky drivers hired to use it. Perhaps a touch small, and lacking in wheel movement, but it was powerful, the lightest, most nimble, and best financed of all. With works support withdrawn at the end of 1992, it was now past its peak. After recording eight World victories in 1992, there would be only two second places in 1993, and none after that.

Mitsubishi Lancer Evolution – front transverse-engine, four-wheel drive. The earlier Galant had been too heavy and too large to be a consistent winner, and was not backed by a full-blooded, fully-financed, programme: from 1993, the new, smaller Lancer Evolution was more competitive. Already competitive on loose-surface/rough-road events when driven by top-grade drivers, thoughthe signing of these drivers was delayed due to parsimonious management policies. Mitsubishi, like Subaru, was a team for the future, still to build a reputation. Galants had won six World events by 1992, most of them on endurance events. From 1995, though, the team's major advantage was that Tommi Makinen would join them as their lead driver. It was not until he left to drive for Subaru was that Mitsubishi's winning sequence ended.

the minimum weight limits which applied: In some cases this was done so easily that ballast could be applied to redistribute the minimum weight. Inventive engineers could see ways of circumventing turbocharger restrictions, and some undoubtedly did so ...

By the time the Impreza WRX/Turbo was homologated (on 1 April 1993), Nissan had withdrawn, and this was the line up of Subaru's four major competitors:

Ford Escort RS Cosworth – front in-line engine, four-wheel drive. First seen as a prototype in 1990, and effectively based on a short-platform Sierra Cosworth 4x4, with smaller Escort-style coachwork and extravagant aerodynamic aids. Benefitting from every Sierra development and experience, it was already a World rally winner. Widely seen as having the best basic layout of all contenders, and being a potential winner on all surfaces. Drawbacks? Ford lacked the finance and perhaps the total commitment to beat the rest of the world. Even so, this car would win five World events in its

Toyota Celica Turbo 4WD – front transverse-engine, four-wheel drive. As the Delta Integrale went into decline, the latest Celica (first homologated on 1 January 1992) was the standard setter. Powerful, well-engineered (by TTE in Cologne), and seemingly with a limitless budget, the Celica team had won five World rounds in 1992, and would win seven more times in 1993. The driving team – Juha Kankkunen and Didier Auriol – was first-rate, and the team ruthless. Widespread rumours of rule-bending were rarely pursued by scrutineers, though the Celica's astonishing straight-line performance could never be explained by normal analysis.

Retribution would follow in the mid-1990s when the team was caught cheating, and banned from World Rallying for the whole of 1996. No-one in rallying ever suggested that this punishment was too harsh ...

Looking into its crystal ball, Subaru might have known that Mitsubishi's much smaller, lighter and more effective car – the Lancer – would soon set standards, though no-one, surely, could have forecast that Toyota's ST205 Celica team would be disgraced, and would be banned for the whole of 1996. Those, however, were the only major developments to hinder the Impreza's progress in its first four seasons. After that, when the World Rally Car formula came into force, things would become progressively more competitive.

Even so, no-one at Subaru or Prodrive could have foreseen that the Impreza Turbo, the WRC, or other models derived from that original Impreza, would still be winning rallied more than twelve years after the model was first seen.

Homologation – meeting the rules

As far as Subaru was concerned, it was never going to be a problem to make enough cars to meet the Group A regulations. Recently revised, these required 2500 identical cars to be produced within a twelve month period which, as far as Subaru was concerned, was easy-peasy. In 1992, Subaru, which was merely one arm of the giant Fuji Heavy Industries combine, had built 420,000 cars (which was four times that of Lancia's output), and its sales force had no qualms about producing a rather special turbocharged Impreza.

When the Impreza Turbo (WRX In other territories) went on sale in the UK, we could all see why this was so. In mid-1993, at a time when the stripped-out version of the new Ford Escort RS Cosworth had just been launched at £22,500, the Impreza Turbo retailed for a mere £17,499. It was as fast as the Ford, as sure-footed as the Ford, and backed by the same sort of rallying ambitions as the Ford – no wonder that enthusiasts flocked into Subaru showrooms to place their orders. Within months, Subaru's problem was not to sell the cars, but to satisfy the waiting lists.

Because the Impreza was in any case, based on the same engine, four-wheel drive transmission and suspension systems as the longer-established Legacy, it had hit the ground running after being launched in October 1992. The 16-valve turbocharged 2-litre version of the flat-4 engine was available from day one, and was actively promoted in all markets.

The Impreza Turbo, in other words, was no 'homologation special', nor a car which had been reluctantly developed by a company needing to indulge its motorsport arm. Whereas Ford, and to a lesser degree, Lancia, produced a car intended for motorsport, and which was neither likely to be sold in big numbers, nor to be honestly profitable in the long term, the Impreza Turbo was a mainstream production car with 208bhp @ 6000rpm (ultra-special versions with 250bhp were sold in Japan) and a choice of ratios in a 5-speed manual transmission.

Ford's Escort RS Cosworth would be on sale for four years, in diminishing quantities, where the Impreza Turbo, and its descendants, would not only sell better with every year that passed, but would also give rise to a multitude of more specialised, higher-powered, special editions. There would also be a new-generation model in 2000. Homologation, therefore, was never likely to be a problem. Production began during the winter of 1992/93, and Group A Homologation of a car titled 'Subaru Impreza 555' was achieved on 1 April 1993, well before Prodrive was ready to start using the car in World rallying.

Thereafter, Prodrive got down to the serious business of making a good car into a great car, then a greater car and – by the end of the 1990s – virtually the world's most successful World Rally Car. Even the first rally cars would have well over 300bhp and a 6-speed transmission option, The truly important statistics, though, were that the newly homologated car was 7.7in/5mm shorter than the now-obsolete Legacy, could comfortably be brought down to the minimum weight limit, and could even carry ballast to further trim the handling.

Engineering features

Although rally development of the Subaru and all its successors was concentrated at the ultra-modern Prodrive complex in Banbury, the initial design, basic engineering, and primary rally development was, of course, completed by Subaru at Shinjuku-ku in Japan.

By most motor industry standards Subaru was a very 'young' manufacturer. Although Fuji Heavy Industries Ltd already had interests in aircraft, railways, agriculture, shipbuilding, buses, and light commercial vehicles before it produced its first car, the tiny 356cc-engined 360, in 1958. Production and sales of the 360 prospered, such that annual Subaru assembly passed 100,000 in 1968.

The very first sporty Subaru model (the Leone) appeared in 1971, soon afterwards the first four-wheel drive Subaru appeared in 1972 (an estate car really intended for agricultural use in what we nowadays call 'soft-road' conditions), and it wasn't long before Subaru's four-wheel drive types (mainly used in light commercial vehicles and otherwise humble family cars) were making up more than one third of the brand's output. At the end of the 1980s, however, Subaru moved firmly up-market by launching the Sierra-sized Legacy, a car which featured new generations of two now traditional Subaru features – a front-mounted, water-cooled, flat-4 engine, and a remarkably advanced four-wheel drive installation.

It was from that new platform that a new and rather smaller car, the Impreza, would be developed, not only as a direct replacement for the long-running Leone range, but to move the brand even further up-market. The Impreza Turbo/WRX, around which the works rally team's long-term strategy was to be centred, was always part of that range.

Rally car layout

By the early 1990s, any manufacturer who wanted to produce a car that could win World events had to comply with the FIA's wishes. A combination of regulations, a sliding scale of minimum weights which were related to engine capacity, and the FIA's tacit requirement that rally cars should not have more than 300bhp at this level, meant that every competitive car had a turbocharged 2-litre engine, complete with four-wheel drive, and had to have an unladen weight, as prepared, of not less than 1200kg/2646lb.

That '300bhp' figure, incidentally, was always a hopeful figure, rather than a regulatory requirement, and it was not (and could not) be policed by the authorities. Years earlier, someone had persuaded the FIA that turbocharged 2-litre cars could not produce much more than 300bhp, though even in the mid-1980s a race-prepared Ford Sierra RS Cosworth could produce 340bhp in day-in-day-out tune!

By the early 1990s, all competitive rally car engines enjoyed peak outputs in the 350/360bhp region while running on commercially available fuels. Some manufacturers – Lancia and Toyota were two such – worked out how to boost their 2-litre engines to at least 400bhp, but this could only be done by using illegal fuel additives.

Even while the Impreza was being developed, the FIA was becoming alarmed at the way that such Group A power outputs continued to increase, and was already discussing ways of capping them. From the start of 1990, turbocharged cars had been obliged to run with 40mm diameter restrictors up-stream of the turbocharger unit itself, and the FIA also stated that it would not change that situation until the end of 1994. Later, and as many rallying cynics had long forecast that it would, the FIA reneged on this ruling, by announcing the 38mm diameter restrictors would be standardised for 1992 (and 36mm for Group N cars). Engines would be further throttled for 1995 when that turbo restrictor dimension was reduced to 34mm/32mm respectively.

Because Prodrive was actively campaigning the Legacy RS by this time, Subaru kept abreast of these trends. While the original works Impreza's engine produced comfortably in excess of the quoted 300bhp, work on making it cope with a turbocharger restrictor had taken time – just think how powerful it might have been without a restrictor!

In many ways, Subaru and Ford were both progressing their rally car policies in the same manner. Starting on the basis of an already-proven car, they would both produce a smaller, lighter, and more nimble machine to replace it. In Ford's case, the Sierra Cosworth 4x4 had been the donor car for the Escort RS Cosworth (which began its career in the same season as the Impreza), while at Subaru the Legacy RS was the proven and accomplished donor car for the Impreza.

There was, however, one basic difference – Ford only produced the smaller Escort RS Cosworth in limited numbers, and one model, for motorsport, while Subaru produced the Impreza as an entirely new and comprehensive range. When the Impreza was homologated, therefore, there were other versions with saloon and estate car bodies, some with front-wheel drive, but most with four-wheel drive, with single-overhead-camshaft and twin-overhead-camshaft engines ranging from 1.5-litres to 2-litres, from 90bhp to 240bhp, and with manual or automatic transmission – all of them already established and proven in the Legacy range.

Flat-4 engines

Like almost every other basic engineering feature of the motor car, the first flat-4 cylinder engines were produced a full century ago, but were rarely used in private cars until the 1930s. That was the decade in which Dr Ferdinand Porsche engineered the air-cooled KDF-Wagen which eventually became the VW Beetle, while in the UK Jowett produced a water-cooled flat-4 in 1936 (which accompanied the flat-twin engines it had been producing for so long. After the war Jowett would go on to produce a brand-new 1½-litre engine for its Javelin family saloon. In the meantime, air-cooled flat-4 engines were introduced into light aircraft in the 1930s – these and logical flat-6 derivatives becoming the norm in later years.

By the 1950s, the Beetle, the powerful Porsche flat-4, and the Jowett which had evolved from it, had proved several points, both for and against the layout. Although it was acknowledged as one of the most compact ways to package four cylinders around one crankshaft, it was also apparent that it was quite an expensive way of providing a given engine capacity.

The packaging bonus was considerable, especially at the front, where a flat-4 engine was easily capable of being fitted in-between the wheelarch panels for the front wheels, and its low overall height was a distinctive advantage in providing low-down weight (good for handling), and allowing for the possibility of having a low front end (good for reducing aerodynamic drag).

If the crankshaft and main bearing layout was carefully arranged, a flat-4 engine could be well-balanced, and robust. The biggest problem facing any manufacturer, however, was one of cost. In an industry dominated by the habit of producing straight-4, straight-6, and V8 engines, the problems, and cost, or arranging to make flat-4 engines were considerable, especially as it was necessary to provide two cylinder heads instead of one, and usually two half-block/crankcases instead of one, along with other related complications. If overhead camshaft cylinder heads were to be chosen, that also meant providing two camshafts, and two camshaft drives, instead of one.

Subaru's first ever flat-4 engine was the 977cc engine of the FF-1, which was introduced in 1966.

As with all rally cars of this era, the Impreza was based on a solid, conventional, unit-construction body/chassis monocoque, this having four-passenger doors and a rounded style. The platform (what traditionalists might have called the 'chassis') section of this monocoque was no more and no less than a shortened version of that used in the existing Legacy, though the reduction was more in overall length than in wheelbase. The Impreza's wheelbase was 99.2in/2520mm, compared with the 101.5in/2580mm of the Legacy, a reduction of only 2.3in/60mm – though in overall length the Impreza was 7.7in/5mm shorter.

Under the skin, the Legacy's unique layout was carried forward to the Impreza, by having the flat-4 water-cooled engine mounted entirely ahead of the front axle line. Because of the engine's layout, and the fact that all the castings were in light alloy, this meant that the centre of gravity of the car was most commendably low. Although this unique engine layout meant that the nose had to be a little longer than some of the obvious rivals, it also meant that the Impreza probably had superior traction to some of them.

Estimates for the static/unladen weight distribution of the car put this at 55 per cent front/45 per cent rear, which was slightly better balanced than the Legacy's distribution (58 per cent/42 per cent) had been. The forward-biased weight tendency was inescapable, due to the way the engine was positioned. Because so much of the Impreza's running gear was a long way up front, this gave Prodrive every chance to mount extra rally gear amidships or even further towards the rear to balance it. This wasn't a particularly light car – independent road tests put the half-full fuel tank weight at 2675lb/1213kg, but Prodrive was confident that it could easily get the car down to minimum regulation weights in due course.

Suspension, steering and braking was all a further development of the Legacy layout, with carefully-matched coil spring/MacPherson strut independent suspensions at front and rear, with power-assisted rack-and-pinion steering, and with big disc brakes at all four-wheels. Everything, it seems, was basically right to start with, so Prodrive's rally development engineers would certainly not have to spend months ironing out any basic problems – because there did not seem to be any.

Prodrive, in any case, had been involved in the development of the most powerful Imprezas well over two years before the car even broke cover. Well before the end of 1990 (when the Impreza's 'parent', the Legacy, was still finding its feet in motorsport), Prodrive had been consulted by STI on the layout of the Impreza WRX, on details of the way that weight could be reduced, of where and how air should be channelled into, and out of, the crowded engine bay, and where the all-important intercooler should be located. Because the rest of the Impreza's running gear was to be so closely based on that of the Legacy, the engine/transmission/engine bay area could be carefully studied to get the very best out of it.

Engine

Before the Legacy arrived in 1990, no serious rally team had ever before used a water-cooled flat-4 engine. Previous 'flat' engines had all been air-cooled, and found in VWs (flat-4) and in Porsche 914/6 and 911 models (flat-6). Along with its descendant, the Impreza, therefore, this extended family of Subarus was unique in rallying terms.

Although water-cooled flat-4 engines were by no means unknown on production cars (Jowett, of all people, had used such a layout on the Javelin in the 1940s and 1950s), it was only Subaru who used such engines in more modern times. First-generation (and much simpler) Subaru flat-4s, with aluminium castings, but with conventional overhead valve gear, had appeared in the 1000 model in 1966, but the engine revealed for the Legacy in 1989 was of a new family.

Still all-aluminium (which was expensive to build, but was smooth and easy to balance), this was a sturdy new design, the EJ series. Although all models had 16 valves, the 'base' models (even up to the 2-litre/115bhp power units) had single overhead camshaft cylinder heads, though normally-aspirated 2-litre types had 150bhp and twin overhead camshafts.

It was this engine which Subaru chose to turbocharge

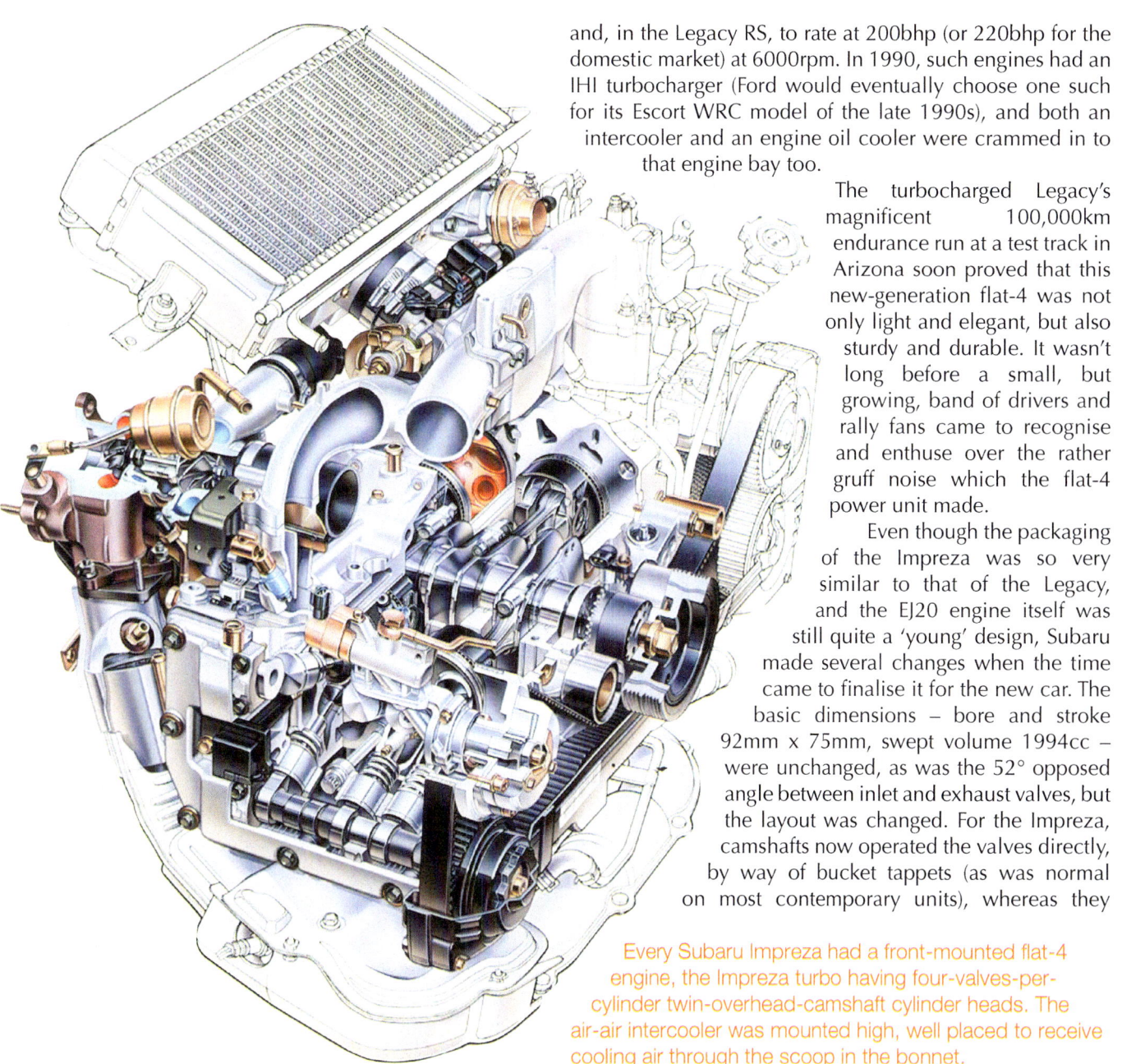

and, in the Legacy RS, to rate at 200bhp (or 220bhp for the domestic market) at 6000rpm. In 1990, such engines had an IHI turbocharger (Ford would eventually choose one such for its Escort WRC model of the late 1990s), and both an intercooler and an engine oil cooler were crammed in to that engine bay too.

The turbocharged Legacy's magnificent 100,000km endurance run at a test track in Arizona soon proved that this new-generation flat-4 was not only light and elegant, but also sturdy and durable. It wasn't long before a small, but growing, band of drivers and rally fans came to recognise and enthuse over the rather gruff noise which the flat-4 power unit made.

Even though the packaging of the Impreza was so very similar to that of the Legacy, and the EJ20 engine itself was still quite a 'young' design, Subaru made several changes when the time came to finalise it for the new car. The basic dimensions – bore and stroke 92mm x 75mm, swept volume 1994cc – were unchanged, as was the 52° opposed angle between inlet and exhaust valves, but the layout was changed. For the Impreza, camshafts now operated the valves directly, by way of bucket tappets (as was normal on most contemporary units), whereas they

Every Subaru Impreza had a front-mounted flat-4 engine, the Impreza turbo having four-valves-per-cylinder twin-overhead-camshaft cylinder heads. The air-air intercooler was mounted high, well placed to receive cooling air through the scoop in the bonnet.

had been operated via fingers on the Legacy. Breathing improvements, improvements to the IHI turbocharger, and the use of a larger and more efficient air-air intercooler allowed the road cars to be sold with 208 or even 250bhp (home market only) @ 6000rpm. This, for the time being, meant that the Impreza would be the most powerful of all the rally-intended 'homologation specials' to be put on sale.

As far as motorsport was concerned, the layout of the EJ20 was near perfect. Not only was it light, compact, and low-mounted, but because of the heavily over-square layout and the 16-valve twin-cam layout, it was almost crying out for further modification and power-tuning in Group A form. Because Prodrive had been consulted at early stage, even when the engine was producing more than 300bhp, Subaru had already worked out how to keep the air circulating in and out of the engine bay. This was important, for even as this car was being prepared, Subaru's rival, Nissan, was suffering repeated embarrassment over the engine/intercooler layout in the new Sunny GTi-R 'homologation special': because the intercooler in that car sat atop the engine, in certain conditions it was unable to do its job properly and was cynically dubbed the 'interwarmer'.

Transmission

For the Impreza road car, Subaru naturally chose a 'full-time' four-wheel drive installation. Because of the layout of the Legacy/Impreza motor car, the entire engine was ahead of the line of the front wheels, with the bulk of the transmission therefore in line or behind that line. From there, and absolutely on the centre line of the car, a two-piece propeller shaft led back to the chassis-mounted rear differential.

Clearly Subaru wanted this car to be suitable for Group N as well as Group A rallying. According to authoritative European dictionaries/buyers' guides of the period, there were no fewer than three different sets of 5-speed ratios, that exclusively intended for the Japanese market models being the most promising. On the road cars, the transmission itself split its torque 50 per cent front/50 per cent rear, but all manner of variations were available in Group A tune.

Outboard of all this, the Turbo had purposeful-looking 16in five-spoke alloy wheels, with 6.0in rim width and 205/55-section tyres – not, perhaps, as extreme as the Escort RS Cosworth of the period (which had 8.0in rims) – but still a good basis around which to build the specification of a rally car. When the Prodrive cars started rallying they used gold-painted Speedline wheels of 16in or 17in diameter, in a variety of rim widths; these looked remarkably like the road wheels, but were totally different in every detail besides appearance.

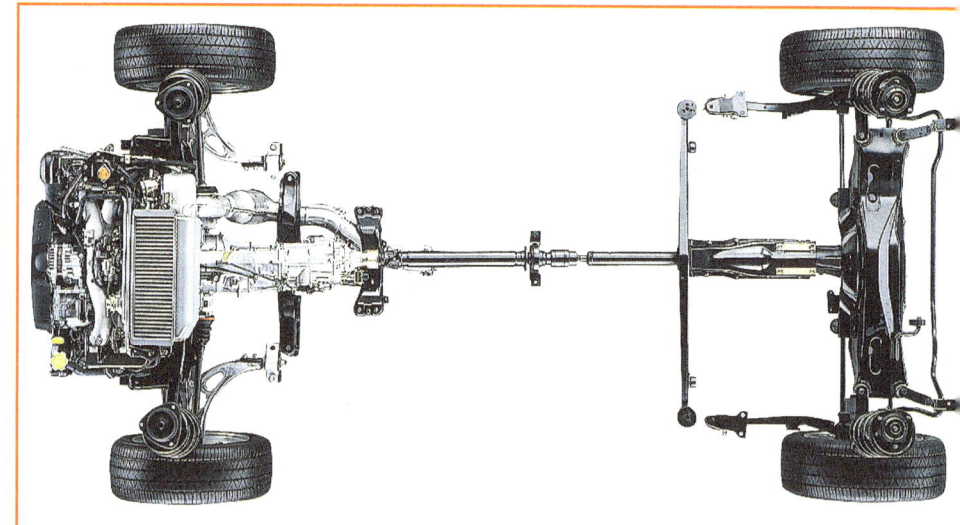

This truly excellent general arrangement of the Impreza's four-wheel drive transmission shows how the flat-4 engine was mounted in the extreme nose, with the main transmission between driver and passenger footwells, and the beautifully packaged independent rear suspension in the tail.

Carlos Sainz charging through a watersplash on the 1994 RAC rally.

Bodyshell

Outwardly at least, the new Impreza was a typically conventional four-door saloon, and (unlike the Ford Escort RS Cosworth), there were few obvious or flamboyant aerodynamic aids. Like the older and larger Legacy, in fact, this car had quite an understated style in every way, all curves and neat proportions, not angular or brutal in any aspect.

Subaru, however, had thought through the air-flow characteristics as carefully as possible. Compared with

Lining up to start the Tour de Corse in 1995 – where team cars would take fourth, fifth and sixth on this serpentine event.

other Imprezas, the Turbo had much-enlarged front-end air intakes (including a prominent grille in the front corner of each wing, close to an extra low-mounted driving lamp), along with an enlarged though basically cosmetic boot lid spoiler. This, incidentally, was the only one of the original Impreza range to have an aluminium bonnet pressing, which incorporated a large forward-facing cold-air scoop in the bonnet, immediately atop the air-air-intercooler which added so much to the charge efficiency of this engine. In addition, two other slatted grilles in that bonnet top all helped to keep the engine bay well-ventilated.

All these changes were tested, in private and in public, before the definitive car was ready. A much carved-about Legacy, with a shorter wheelbase, and dubbed 2.0 TZ 4WD, was tested on Safari territory to compare it with the performance of existing Legacy rally cars. Although Subaru admitted nothing at the time, this now appears to have been a serious proving run, to re-assure it that its thoughts on the Impreza WRX were correct – which they were!

Homologation and running changes

Although the Impreza 555 was not homologated until April 1993, much useful rally work had already been done to the power train, running gear and suspension on the Legacy which preceded it. Prodrive's own 6-speed 'dog' gearbox had been developed with that car in mind – and would clearly be useful in the Impreza,

By 1991 Prodrive had produced 17in wheels and massive 14in brakes, hydraulic control of differentials had been further refined, and there was progress with water-

World Rally Cars – a revolution in the sport

Except in rare cases, rallies have always been run for cars which have been 'homologated' (ie 'approved') for use in motorsport. In every case, homologation into a particular category depended on the number of cars built, or at least claimed to have been built.

In the 1960s, almost all world-class rallies were run for cars in Group 2 (saloons, of which 1000 had been built), or Group 3 (500 GT or sports cars). In the 1970s, more and more events were run for Group 4 cars (500-off, later 400-off, any type of car).

The first revolution came in 1982, when Group B (200-off, very special limited-production machines), Group A (5000-off closed cars, considerable modifications allowed), or Group N (5000-off closed cars, virtually no modifications) took over instead. After a series of fatal accidents in 1986, Group B was annulled.

Groups A and N then carried on until the mid 1990s – and to remain competitive, it became essential for cars to have more than 300bhp, and sophisticated four-wheel drive. The Subaru Impreza was typical of this type of car.

However, even though the Group A production requirement was halved in 1992, to 2500 cars, various manufacturers (principally Citroën and Peugeot) complained that they could not justify the investment needed to develop new cars to be competitive with machines like the Impreza, the Ford Escort RS Cosworth, the Toyota Celica GT-Four and the Mitsubishi Lancer.

After much lobbying, the FIA agreed to inaugurate a new category – World Rally Cars – where twenty identical kits capable of being built into complete cars would gain approval. All such cars would have turbocharged 2-litre engines and four-wheel drive, but could be based on much more mundane machines, as long as more than 25,000 of those were built every year.

Even though the FIA granted certain exemptions in the early years, this completely changed the face of World rallying. Subaru produced the Impreza World Rally Car as a natural (and perfectly sporting-legal) evolution of the two-door Impreza, as did Toyota of its mass-market Corolla. For the time being, though, the FIA approved certain exemptions – Ford got away with an evolution of its 2500/year (not 25,000/year) Escort RS Cosworth, while Mitsubishi carried on running a Group A car in WRC-classified events for some years: Ford regularised that situation with the new Focus WRC in 1999.

The requirement on WRC numbers to be built was reduced to only ten cars a year in the early 2000s – which meant that most serious WRC manufacturers (like Subaru, which produced many more than that number of new cars in a year) could afford to build a new model every year.

These two shots show that the Subaru World Rally Car of 1997 was different in almost every detail from the now obsolete Impreza Turbo. Not only the front ...

cooled brakes and a semi-automatic gearchange system. A semi-automatic transmission was homologated on 1 January 1992, and though a fully automatic version was homologated in April 1992, it was not then used.

The Impreza, therefore, entered rallying with virtually a settled mechanical specification, for in all but minor detail it could use the latest iteration of what had proved to be right for the last of the Legacy types. Complete with the sturdy 6-speed gearbox alternatives, the choice of an hydraulically-assisted semi-automatic gearchange (with buttons on the extremity of the steering wheel) or a normal manual change, and with 17in wheels and other tweaks, it was already formidably competitive. By 1995 the engine had needed a complete redevelopment package to suit the compulsory 34mm turbo restrictor – Subaru, like its rivals, found that it had to change camshaft profiles and re-programme its ECUs – while to

... but also the tail, complete with two-door instead of four-door shell, had been updated. World Rally Cars won both the pictured events – Colin McRae the Tour de Corse, Piero Liatti the Monte.

suit these different engines there were different gear ratio alternatives, and, from mid-season, water-injection was added to the engine inlet manifold, which helped produce a little more power.

Other teams were even more frustrated with engine restrictions. It was in 1995, please note, that Toyota was found to have evolved a totally illegal method of channelling more air into the engine, by cleverly bypassing the restrictor/turbocharger casting assembly to produce a lot more power. The result was that all its Championship points were withdrawn by the FIA, and it was banned from rallying until 1997.

Few major changes were made in 1996, for, throughout the season, STI (in Japan) and Prodrive (in the UK) were working hard to have their new World Rally Car ready for launch. That car duly made its first appearance in November

1996, and would be ready for its first event, the Monte Carlo Rally, in January 1997.

Impreza World Rally Car

Because the FIA had comprehensively 'moved the goalposts', Subaru had been able to take a long, hard look at the turbocharged Impreza, and to up-rate its specification to suit the new 2-litre formula. Under World Rally Car rules, cars had to be based on a production vehicle of which at least 25,000 were being built in any year, though turbocharging, four-wheel drive and other features could all be added, and only 20 identical kits of parts to build cars had to be produced before homologation was assured. In the Impreza's case, where the team itself had a demand for almost that number of new cars in a hectic season, and others could certainly be provided to other teams in Europe, and in the Asia-Pacific countries, this meant that a new and improved version could be produced in almost every succeeding year.

In this case, Prodrive did much of the engineering and development work on the new car, although as ever there was the closest possible co-operation with the STI division of Subaru back in Japan. To meet FIA regulations, when the inspectors came to call, Prodrive had to show a complete road car, a complete as-intended rally car, a fully-prepared bodyshell complete with all the 'closures' (doors, bonnet and boot), and the balance of the special body panels and rally mechanical parts needed to make up those numbers.

One important new provision was that a chassis number/VIN code was now rigidly linked to a bodyshell/roll cage assembly, which meant a battered old car could no longer be re-shelled. Functionally this did not affect Subaru, but it meant that the now-famous series of 'personalised' registration numbers had to be abandoned. Instead, Prodrive began using an ever-lengthening ' ... WRC', and eventually ' ... SRT' series instead.

When the Impreza WRC was revealed in Spain, in November 1996, it was clear that almost every aspect of the 'base' car had been studied and, where possible, modified: team boss David Richards claimed that there were at least 50 new elements in the car which differed from, and improved on, the original rallying package. With STI's backing, Prodrive had no qualms about making these models extra-special (and usually, by definition, high-cost), because only 20 sets had to be produced to ensure WRC homologation.

Work had begun in February 1996, exterior re-shaping had begun in March (but was not finalised for twelve weeks), and the first of the new-type cars had been completed early in October. Colin McRae had already driven the car and made development suggestions before it was packed up for dispatch to Spain, where it was launched to the Press immediately before the start of the Rally Catalunya.

In conjunction with STI in Japan, not only had Prodrive's David Lapworth searched diligently for improvements on the existing Subaru 555, but styling guru Peter Stevens had been hired to do the seemingly impossible – to make the new version look fiercer and more purposeful than before, but to make it more aerodynamically efficient. In the event, even the sponsor's '555' decals were more rakish than before ...

These were the principal changes:

Bodyshell

Although the basic profile of the car was as before, for the very first time here was a two-door Impreza rally car. To meet the regulations (which stated that WRCs had to be based on a car of which 25,000 were being produced every year, Subaru claimed that the new car was based on the Coupé or Retna model, which ran on precisely the same platform and wide choice of flat-4-engined running gear. This derivative had been on sale since 1994, but not in full-blown Turbo form. Because the same rules allowed complete engine turbocharging, transmission and other mechanical changes, plus aerodynamic enhancements, this was ideal for Subaru's purposes.

Visual changes were obvious, but other aerodynamic improvements were hidden away, and not discussed. The front end was at once simpler and more functional than the donor car, with larger cross-sectional areas to get air into the engine bay and towards the front brakes. The lower front spoiler was more prominent than before. The bonnet panel, complete with cold air scoop, now had

Showing off its large cooling air intakes to the engine bay, Colin McRae's Impreza World Rally Car on its way to winning the 1998 Rally of Portugal.

larger louvres to each side of that, and flared wheelarches allowed wider-track/wider-rim wheels to be used. Wider cars – up to 96.6in/1770mm – were foreseen under the new WRC regulations so manufacturers designing new models took advantage of the new limits for, by definition, a wider wheel track theoretically meant that the machine was more stable. Theoretically or actually? It was up to Prodrive's development engineers to make sure of that ...

Crowd control? What crowd control? These were the primitive conditions that the Prodrive team had to face on the Safari.

At the rear, not only was there a larger and more functional transverse boot-lid spoiler, but flared rear arches to match those at the front, and a rear bumper moulding shaped effectively to match the front. A larger transmission tunnel allowed more cooling air to flow under the car, especially around the gearbox. Finally, when Stevens and Lapworth were satisfied, a mock-up of the new car was taken to MIRA for aerodynamic assessment in the wind tunnel. This was, in other words, a thoroughly grown-up version of the now-obsolete Subaru Turbo rally car, and was expected to be more effective. Although Prodrive would not quantify the improvements, it was happy to claim that, at speed, the WRC produced downforce, whereas the Turbo (555) had produced lift: this promised more stability and more security for the drivers, who were looking forward to proving the point.

Naturally there was a revised and more rigid roll cage, plus sturdy side-impact protection in the doors (by lightweight honeycomb panels), along with glass-fibre panels fitting into the inboard side of the roll cage itself.

Engine

Because the new rules allowed a much larger intercooler to be used (up to nine litres in volume), Prodrive made a major change and relocated that component to the front of the engine bay, ahead of the water radiator, from its old less-than-ideal place behind and above the engine. In addition, and for environmental reasons, new regulations required a catalytic converter to be fitted in the exhaust system.

Less obvious was the fact that the engine was moved slightly back in the chassis. There was also a complete redesigning of the inlet manifold, and a slight re-alignment of the turbocharger, both to suit the relocation of the intercooler. Ducting and piping to, from and around the engine was at once more obviously placed, and more efficient than before, and though Lapworth agreed that there had been a power improvement, he would not say how much!

For the new car, Subaru quoted a peak of 300bhp @ 5500rpm – peak power had been developed at 6500rpm on the 555 – with a tiny increase in torque. Even with the compulsory 34mm diameter restrictor up-stream of the turbocharger, peak power was comfortably more than the FIA's suggested 300bhp limit though, like all its rivals, Prodrive/Subaru blandly refused to quote more than 300bhp. Prodrive knew it was a fiction, the FIA knew it was a fiction, and the public knew that it was a fiction – but nothing more was done about it.

Transmission

For the time being Prodrive continued to use the 6-speed semi-automatic main gearbox/transmission that had been designed way back in 1989, and which had been fitted to every works Legacy and every works Impreza 555. Work on a new 6-speeder had, however, been started, and when this was ready it would be available, Lapworth claimed, in H-gate, semi-automatic or sequential form.

Suspension, brakes and chassis

Except that the use of wider wheelarches allowed wider wheel tracks to be used, the only important suspension change was to produce new cross-members and new suspension arms to allow for that wider track. As on the original Imprezas, there was MacPherson strut suspension at front and rear, along with power-assisted rack-and-pinion steering. Over the years, and especially as tracks were widened to take advantage of changing regulations, almost every element of the chassis would be changed. There was virtually no commonality between a 1997 Impreza WRC and a 2005 Impreza WRC – while a car built in the interim period probably differed from both of those cars.

Homologation and running changes

Having produced its 20 sets of parts in 1996/97, which satisfied World Rally Car regulations and were all incorporated in cars during the season, during 1998 Prodrive added another 12 new cars to that list. Not that all of them remained at Banbury, of course, for many of the older machines were sold off after a few events to deserving private teams which could afford to keep them running and, hopefully, to win events at European level.

Newly homologated features for the start of the season included a new type of turbocharger, stronger engine internal components, revised chassis/suspension details and a detachable front 'splitter' for the front spoiler. Splitters, which were useful for trimming the aerodynamic down-force level at the front of the car, had previously been used in saloon car racing, and in Group B cars: Ford's Escort RS Cosworth, homologated in 1993 alongside the original Impreza, had always included such a feature.

Interestingly, the sequential gearbox that David

Visually different from its predecessors, for 1999 the re-homologated Impreza World Rally Car was more competitive than before. Great attention had been paid to getting air into and out of the crowded engine bay. This was Monte Carlo in January, when new recruit Juha Kankkunen took a fine second place.

Lapworth had mentioned (he made this promise at the end of 1996) was still not yet ready for use in rallying.

Other features added during the year were strengthened damper mountings, a successful 'fix' for that old bug-bear, the camshaft pulley failure problem, and the use of active differentials in all three positions. Perhaps it was because the 1998 car was technically disappointing that, as early as August of that year, Colin McRae made a decision to leave the team – he would join Ford to drive the all-new Focus in 1999.

Although the Impreza was re-homologated for 1999, the cars were still painted blue with yellow livery markings; the major visual change was that Subaru's own multi-star logos had replaced the 555 markings (familiar between 1993 and 1998). Different wheel styles were sometimes in evidence, and there was a lighter yet stiffer safety roll cage, but the structure was much as before. Engines were still officially rated at 300bhp @ 5500rpm, but much work went into refining the gear change, including a combination of electrical and hydraulic actuation of the gear change (in place of the original mechanical linkage). Triple active differentials were now normal wear. Bigger and more powerful six-pot brakes were eventually adopted, and there was now such a wide choice of narrow, medium and wide-track suspensions that the drivers often seemed to confuse themselves. Because the intercooler was in the nose, cool air was no longer needed through the bonnet scoop ahead of the screen, so this was now blanked off: along with larger air outlets close to the nose, this made the bonnet look rather different from the earlier cars.

For 2000 (and the WRC200 derivative), technical chief Christian Loriaux had spent much time optimising the Subaru's layout, his two priorities apparently being to lose weight where it was at all possible, and to drop every component towards the ground where at all possible. Launched early in the year, this fourth iteration was used for the first time in Portugal in March. Visually it was little changed, except around the nose, where there were to be two separate intakes (one for the cooling radiator, one for the intercooler), for most updates were mechanical and hidden away. Fundamental to this was a re-jig of the inner bodyshell, roll cage, and fuel tank, the tank being smaller, saddle-shaped and lower down to reduce the centre of gravity.

Water, lots of it, in Argentina 1999, with Juha Kankkunen charging through it on his way to winning the event. By this time the Impreza World Rally Car could deal with almost all road and rally conditions.

Although the power and torque rating of the flat-4 turbocharged engine was officially unchanged, the location of the turbocharger, the manifolds and the ducting had been changed, while there were also changes to air-flow management in the engine bay. A reshuffle put the water radiator lower in the shell, with the air-air intercooler now on top of it. Suspension components were lighter and new, and the rear cross-member was much changed.

New shell for 2001

The next major change for the rally team came in January 2001, when the fifth version of the Impreza WRC was homologated. Although the existing platform, suspensions and basic running gear of the earlier car were all retained, this car did have a new style, and mostly smoother lines with more glass area. The bodyshell was claimed to be much stiffer than before (Subaru claimed that road cars were 185 per cent more resistant to torsion, and 250 per cent better in bending), but to some people this new machine also had an awkwardly styled nose, with bulkier headlamp pods including the fashionable small projectors (by

Look carefully under Richard Burns' Impreza WRC, and you can see the full length skid shielding which all modern WRCs needed to keep their precious engines and drivetrains in one piece. This was Australia 1999, the scene of Burns' second victory of the season.

The familiar shape of Subaru's 2000-style Impreza World Rally Car, with Richard Burns on his way to winning the Rally of Great Britain.

For 2001, Subaru completely re-developed the Impreza World Rally Car, to keep up with road car trends. This was Monte Carlo in January, where the Prodrive team reverted to the four-door bodyshell, a new headlamp treatment, and many technical changes under the skin.

Few other rally cars looked quite as purposeful as the Impreza WRC – and, in his first drive for the team, Tommi Makinen found it effective, too.

this time, rally cars tended to keep 'office hours', so good lighting performance was no longer vital), and a revised, larger and more effective rear aerofoil.

Once again, this was a specialised Prodrive rally car derivative which had been shaped by specialist Peter Stevens (a job completed just before he took up the thankless job of design consultant to the MG-Rover business at Longbridge), so it looked just as aggressive and purposeful as one expected.

Critically, though, this was the first Impreza WRC to feature four doors (the original Impreza WRC of 1993-96 had used four doors too, so this was a reversion to original practice), that style being accompanied by yet another variation of aluminium bonnet style/air intakes/scoop layout. Much of the development work first seen in the 2000 Prodrive car was carried over, but throughout the year there was continual development under the bonnet, connected with air-flow management into/out of and around the flat-4 engine. Repeatedly, and frustratingly there were electronic problems to be solved ("you can't see electricity", as one observer commented).

By using all the features of the now obsolete Impreza WRC of 2000, the weight was kept down, not only in total, but towards the ground. Before ballast was added, the works cars were invariably lighter than the official minimum weight limit of 2706lb/1230kg.

Changes for 2002 were limited, and did not surface until Corsica in March. They were concentrated on a lighter but stronger engine flywheel, a revised exhaust manifold and a revised engine water-injection system. Visually there was a larger front lower spoiler/splitter moulding, and improvements to cockpit ventilation that included a revised roof vent. Otherwise, the engineers concentrated on more major changes for 2003.

Once again the Impreza WRC was re-homologated for 2003, this car carrying evidence of much more STI influence from Japan. There were several obvious and (as experience proved) successful aerodynamic improvements, including yet more modifications to the front end/moulding/bonnet panel area, and yet another headlamp arrangements (the same as the latest production cars). At the rear, there was a new transverse spoiler, complete with four intermediate 'fences' between the end slats.

The engine was once again re-packaged, with a new turbocharger, exhaust manifold and other internal changes. Because this was a car which could easily get down to the minimum weight limit, the opportunity was taken up to beef up some suspension and mounting components and, because of a change in rear suspension geometry, there was a marginal increase in wheelbase. This was the season when a form of 'active' suspension damper control was first used, though not on every occasion.

The 2004 iteration of the long-running Impreza was ready in March (and the Rally of Mexico), most changes

This atmospheric shot shows both works Impreza WRCs being fettled on the Rally of Great Britain in 2002. X9 SRT, in the foreground, is Petter Solberg's car, which would win, while Tommi Makinen's sister machine is under the awnings.

being made out of sight. Aerodynamic improvements at the front included revised front mouldings, and the addition of large air intakes (to cool the brakes) ahead of the front wheels, with revised cooling radiator/intercooler positions and ducting. Bodyshell changes included the use of lightweight panels, and polycarbonate windows – and even more ballast than usual could be employed.

There were yet more engine changes, which resulted in significantly more torque, though no more than the 'official' 300bhp rating. (By this time, most WRC teams had managed to extract at least 320bhp from engines throttled by a 34mm turbo restrictor, but to keep the FIA happy no-one ever admitted to this.)

This car carried on into the start of the 2005 season,

On only his second visit to Mexico, Petter Solberg took his Impreza WRC to a serene victory in 2005, temporarily leading the Drivers' Championship standings as a result. Note – that rear aerofoil may look flamboyant, but it was also extremely effective.

after which yet another version of this long-running car was homologated. By the end of that year, no fewer than eleven of the new machines had been used. Compared with the 2004 models, there were many evolutionary changes, but nothing startlingly different.

To take advantage of rule changes, the overall width of the latest Impreza went up to the maximum allowable dimension of 70.8in/1800mm, which meant that the maximum track could also be stretched to allow for wider wheel tracks and tyres to be used, and at the same time many different suspension components were introduced.

Under the bonnet, there were more detail changes to the engine, fuel injection, and radiator/cooling arrangements. To match all this there was a new lower front-end panel moulding, along with revisions to the transmission hydraulic control system, and a different type of water-cooling layout for the brakes.

This confirmed, of course, that either Subaru, or Prodrive, was always dreaming up new ways of optimising the Impreza World Rally Car to meet the ever-tightening technical and homologation regulations. It might be interesting to compare the detail technical specifications of a 1993 Impreza WRX/Turbo against the 2005 Impreza World Rally, to see if there were any components (except for a few nuts and bolts) which had been carried over for twelve years. My guess is – none at all!

Was the Impreza unique?

It all depends on what you mean by 'unique'? Its mechanical layout – matching a front-mounted/water-cooled flat-4 engine to four-wheel drive – was certainly unique, though most other detail features of the design were conventional by any motor industry standards. What made the works Imprezas unique was not that they were so successful, but that they won rallies over such a long period. By the end of 2005, Prodrive cars had won no fewer than 46 World rallies. Although this figure was exactly matched by every iteration of the front-engined Lancia Delta, that car's career is over, and the Impreza looks like adding to its illustrious record in future years.

Model builders would also point out that they know of no other rally car/rally team that retained the same basic gold livery on a blue background for such a long time – so much so that an Impreza would be immediately recognisable, even if all traces of badging were removed.

It was also a car – more specifically a family of closely-related cars – which did more to boost the marketing image of a marque, or marque family, than any car since the legendary Ford Escorts of the 1970s. For Subaru, success in world-level rallying did more to transform the company's standing than any other campaign it attempted. Audi had done the same in the 1980s with the Quattro, but that was a relatively short-lived process.

By 2006, Subaru and Prodrive had woven themselves a real problem for the future; the Impreza had already been around for so long – by 2006 this model had been rallying for more than 12 years – that any really different successor would have a technical and marketing mountain to climb. This is not to say that it could not be achieved – Prodrive has made a habit of delivering on its promises – but it would be a major undertaking. One day, one day ...

Building and running the works cars

Fortunately for Subaru, when Fuji decided to tackle World rallying it took the task seriously, acknowledged that the centre-of-gravity of that sport was in Europe, and concluded that the works team should be based in Europe. We now know that it looked carefully around Europe, realised that three nations – Great Britain, Germany and Italy – were populated by the most credible engineering operations, and wisely settled on the Prodrive operation in the UK.

Although Prodrive eventually became a large, extremely capable, and well-thought-of organisation, it all started as a tiny operation intended to provide an enjoyable living for a rally enthusiast called David Richards. In the 1970s Richards had been a successful rally co-driver who guided Ari Vatanen to win the World Drivers' Championship in 1981 in a Rothmans-backed Ford Escort RS1800. Having set up David Richards Autosports (DRA) he then took on much sporting promotional work for British American Tobacco,

37

developing his connections with Rothmans and (eventually) the 555 cigarette brands.

Originally based at Silverstone, DRA became Prodrive in 1984, its original work being to prepare and run Rothmans-sponsored rally cars for Porsche. After the move to brand-new premises in Banbury (within sight of the also-new M40 motorway) Prodrive then began building some of the world's most effective BMW M3 race and rally cars. Accordingly, when Subaru began to cast around for a European rallying partner, it soon settled on Prodrive as the ideal choice.

In the 1990s and into the 2000s, Prodrive grew consistently, not only becoming one of Banbury's largest employers, but diversifying into many other branches of motorsport, which included building Ford Mondeo Super Touring Car racers, and Ferrari GT race cars. Prodrive also developed and sold large numbers of Imprezas for Group A and Group N rallying, along with several special edition Imprezas that carried factory approval. David Richards also found time to be the managing director of the Benetton F1 team, and later of the BAR F1 team.

In more recent years, Prodrive acquired the old Lucas-Girling test track near Coventry, and converted it into a viable development facility for many manufacturers who lacked such facilities of their own.

Although Subaru's STI subsidiary did much original design and development work in Japan, its actual rallying activities were mainly confined to domestic and Asia-Pacific regions. Rally-car development, and homologation, was carried out by Prodrive, in Banbury, on its behalf, so that a competitor competing in – say – New Zealand – would rely on Prodrive's experience, expertise, and special parts supply to make sure that the car was always kept up to the moment.

One destructive act of God showed just how resourceful Prodrive's business actually was. On one winter's night at the end of the 1990s, serious and uncontrolled flash flooding of the river Cherwell, which flows across the north corner of Prodrive's grounds, led to several workshops and warehouses being inundated over a weekend when the site was virtually deserted.

As one top manager later pointed out to me, at least ten brand-new Group N Imprezas, awaiting delivery, and worth more than £1 million, had to written off as a result of that flood – yet the shortfall was made up within months. Not only was Prodrive used to dealing in such quantities of cars, but it was capable of building new ones without disturbing the entire business for too long.

Personalities and star drivers
Masaru Katsurada

Katsurada, the father of the Legacy, a long-time technical servant of Subaru, was already general manager of vehicle development at Subaru when the Impreza was conceived, and would later go on to be the chief executive of Subaru's performance division STI.

Originally qualifying in aeronautical engineering at Tokyo University, when he was 24-years-old he joined Subaru in 1966. Originally employed in the body construction department, he became a research engineer two years later, then spent time in the USA, returning to Japan to work on computer-aided projects before joining the vehicle evaluation section, eventually becoming project chief behind the Legacy.

David Richards

If ever there was a human equivalent to the perpetual motion machine, then Prodrive's founder and chairman David Richards was it. Having set up Prodrive in 1984, and secured the Subaru World rally business in 1989, he expanded it into a consistent rally-winning operation by the mid-1990s, yet still found time to run the Benetton F1 operation for a time. Although much of the day-to-day Subaru rally programme was run by David Lapworth, especially after 1997 when he was appointed competition chief, Richards was always the prime mover behind strategy and in moulding the image of the team.

Originally an accountant by training, Richards became a successful rally co-driver in the 1970s, first with Tony Pond in Triumphs, then (more famously) with Ari Vatanen in Rothmans-sponsored Ford Escorts: it was the Escort/

Left to right: Ryuichiro Kuze, Colin McRae, Derek Ringer and David Richards – all king-pins in the early days of the Impreza WRC project. Kuze was president of STi when it was founded in 1989.

Vatanen/Richards combination which won the World Rally Championship for Drivers in 1981.

Having firmed up his commercial and promotional links with British American Tobacco (whose Rothmans brand was one of its most important activities), he then set up David Richards Autosports (DRA), which became Prodrive in 1984. Having prepared Rothmans Porsche 911s for rallying, and BMW M3s for British Touring Car racing, he then joined forces with Subaru. Since then Prodrive has become even larger, and has run major programmes for other concerns, including Ford (Mondeo BTCC cars), and Ferrari (GT race cars).

Companies headed by Richards took over the world marketing and commercial rights to the running of World Championship rallying in the late 1990s, and early in the 2000s he also spent time as the boss of the BAR F1 team. A whirlwind in business for more than a quarter of a century, he showed no signs of drawing back from motorsport, deal-making, or business in general – for in the mid-2000s he was even rumoured to want to start his own-brand of F1 operation.

David Lapworth

Appointed competition chief of the Subaru World Rally team from late 1997, David Lapworth already had much engineering and organisational experience at Prodrive before then. Coventry-born in 1956, when that city was still at the centre of the motor industry, he first became involved in motorsport more than twenty years ago.

His first contact with big time rallying came when he worked with Des O'Dell of Peugeot-Talbot on the Talbot Sunbeam-Lotus programme (Talbot won the Makes' series in 1981), but having met David Richards at that time, he began to work with him even before the Prodrive operation was set up.

Involved in the development of every type of works Subaru rally car – from the original Legacy of 1990, and the first Impreza of 1993 – he was the rally team's technical chief from the early 1990s.

Clearly a deep thinker, along with the team at STI in Japan, he was responsible for the evolution of the Impreza World Rally Car. His exposition of the whole philosophy of World Rally car engineering was published in 1997, in Martin Holmes' *World Rallying 1996-1997*, and was quite masterly. Christian Loriaux, the engineer who went on to join the Ford (M-Sport) rally team, honed all his skills in David's department, but since 2000 Lapworth was in complete technical control of all the continuous work which went into the improvement of the Impreza rally car.

Richard Burns

When Richard Burns collapsed at the wheel of his road car in November 2003 (he was on his way to the start of Rally GB), no-one realised that it spelt the end of his rally career. Although he had just agreed to rejoin Prodrive/Subaru for 2004, he would never drive again and, tragically, he died of a malignant brain tumour in November 2005.

Reading-born in 1971, he was car-mad, and later rally-mad, from a very young age. After tackling his first Rally GB in 1990 in a Peugeot 309, he teamed up with Robert Reid, his inseparable rally partner for the next thirteen years.

His first Subaru successes came in the 1993 British Championship, when his Prodrive Legacy won four of the five events. Prodrive then sent him to tackle the Asia-Pacific Championship, but he defected to Mitsubishi where he drove Lancia Evos from 1995 to 1998 (notching up three victories).

Rejoining Subaru for 1999, as a direct replacement for Colin McRae, Richard became Prodrive's lead driver, and in three seasons (1999-2001) recorded eight further victories. In 1999 and 2000 he was second in the World Drivers' championship, while in 2001 he became World Champion. It seemed a bit hard on Prodrive that he decided he was moving over to Peugeot.

As Prodrive's principal engineer on the Impreza project, David Lapworth was one of the most important characters in the team, and always had a close relationship with driver Petter Solberg. David did not move on until 2006.

Richard Burns, World Rally Champion of 2001 in an Impreza, was one of Britain's folk heroes. Tragically, he died in 2005, when still not at his peak as a rally driver.

Time for celebration at last! At the very end of a gruelling fourteen event World Rally season, Richard Burns finally won his World Drivers' Championship.

Contracts were waved, legal action ensued, and no-one (least of all Richard) came out of this fracas with credit, but in the end he abandoned Subaru, and drove for Peugeot for two years, though he did not settle comfortably into the 206 WRC, and was never to win another rally.

Not easy to know (he had a distrust of many media representatives), and sometimes seen as arrogant in later years, he was never a peoples' hero (unlike Colin McRae, who certainly was ...) – yet no-one ever doubted his driving ability.

Colin McRae

For Colin, motorsport was in the blood, for his father Jimmy was multiple British Rally Champion in the 1980s, and

Left to right: David Richards, Colin McRae, Ryuichiro Kuze, and an FIA Official at the close of the 1995 season, when Colin became World Rally Champion, and Subaru won the Makes Championship.

his brother Alister would also achieve World Rally Driver status. After starting on two wheels in motorcycle trials and scrambles, Colin started rallying in 1986, used a Vauxhall Nova in two World Rallies in 1987, and then became prominent in British rallies in rear-wheel drive and four-wheel drive Ford Sierra RS Cosworths until 1990.

Although his driving style was lurid (not for nothing was he nicknamed 'McCrash'), Prodrive hired him to drive Subaru Legacies in the British Championship (which he won in 1991 and 1992), after which he joined the World Championship team. First in Legacies, then, from mid-1993, in Imprezas, he became a pace-setter, and would remain with Prodrive/Subaru until the end of 1998.

The record shows that he became World Rally Champion

Waiting for his due time to come up, at a time control on the Rally Australia of 1998, is Colin McRae's co-driver Nicky Grist.

in 1995 (he was 27-years-old), and that between 1994 and 1998 he won 16 World events, but that same record also shows that he retired after accident damage on eight other occasions. In many ways Colin, and his co-drivers Derek Ringer (to 1996) and Nicky Grist (from 1997), led a charmed life, for they were indeed lucky to walk away from many of those shunts, which could be of air-crash proportions.

Although Prodrive humoured these regular budget-busting excursions, it only did it because he was likely to win next time out – but it must certainly have cost a fortune to keep him in competitive machinery.

Not only did the team warn him about these un-cured kamikaze excursions, but it seems that by 1998 Colin himself wearied of the mechanical failures which still afflicted his cars, and at the end of that season he walked out of Prodrive to join Ford's M-Sport operation in new-style Focus WRC models. One reason, it seems certain, is that Prodrive was not prepared to pay the astronomic fees he had demanded for the future.

After driving for Ford until 2002, he then moved to Citroën for one final season – 2003 – in which he achieved only one podium finish. His contract was not renewed after that (Citroën thought – and it was right – that Sebastian Loeb was a better bet ...) and he was effectively lost to the sport for the next two seasons.

Tommi Makinen

Although the taciturn, often stern-looking Finnish farmer Tommi Makinen was World Champion on four consecutive occasions – 1996 to 1999 inclusive – he seemed only to be completely at ease in the Mitsubishi Lancer Evos which helped give him those crowns. Although his transfer to Subaru/Prodrive, for 2002 and 2003, was amicably achieved, he would only win one event for the Japanese – that being his very first drive: the Monte Carlo rally.

In his early years Tommi drove whatever car was available, but did not settle in a team until 1995. His first World victory was in Finland in 1994 (a works Ford Escort RS Cosworth), after which he joined Mitsubishi in 1995 until 2000: he won no less than twenty World events for that team, moulding the car to his own needs and driving style.

The move 'across town', from Mitsubishi to Subaru, from Rugby to Banbury, came at the end of 2001, when he had suffered a very difficult year with the rival camp. Not only did Prodrive offer him Number One billing ahead of Petter Solberg, it also offered him more technological innovation that Mitsubishi had ever done. That, perhaps, sounded attractive at the time, but in practice it rarely seemed to work out.

In two seasons the quiet and thoughtful Makinen was often out-shone by the extrovert Petter Solberg, his best performances being one victory, one second place and three third places. Accidents and mechanical failures, no doubt, were unsettling, but by mid-2003 (when he was already 39-years-old), the fire went out, and he completed the season at a more gentle pace.

Even so, he retired with everyone's good wishes. In many ways Tommi was a PR man's nightmare, for he never uttered two words if one would suffice, and seemed to prefer silence if at all possible. Letting his driving do the talking, he was always well-liked, but he was happy to retire, sharply and completely, from motorsport at the end of 2003 season.

Carlos Sainz

In an astonishing World rally career, which began in a Ford Sierra RS Cosworth in 1987 and ended in a Citroën Xsara WRC in 2005, Carlos not only won 26 World rallies – more than any other driver – but also gained many friends, millions of admirers, and not a single enemy. The proud Spaniard, Mr – or perhaps I should say Señor – Nice Guy, was totally honest, honourable, and dedicated to whoever was employing him. In the whole of rallying, no-one ever seemed to have a bad word to say about Carlos.

For Carlos, rallying began in Spain in 1980, and he

Tommi Makinen, the quietly-spoken farmer from Finland, had already won four consecutive World Championships before joining the Impreza/Prodrive rally team.

Just how many Tommi Makinens can you get into one Impreza, particularly if one of them is rather stiff and unyielding?

first gained European-wide fame by driving Ford Sierra RS Cosworths in 1987 and 1988. After a four-year spell with Toyota (he became World Champion in 1990 and 1992), he spent an unhappy year with a Jolly Club-run Lancia Delta Integrale before joining Prodrive and the Subaru works team for 1994. It was typical of Carlos that within 24 hours of signing a contract he stepped into an Impreza for the very first time and started offering ideas for its improvement.

For two seasons – 1994 and 1995 – he drove alongside Colin McRae (although he was effectively team leader, the feisty Scot did not seem to acknowledge that) and was quite astonishingly consistent. In 16 World rally starts in Imprezas, he won four rounds, took four second, two third and two fourth places, and retired from the other events, only once due to having an accident. This was an amazing record, as his many followers always expected, and it would surely

'King Carlos' Sainz, a very popular member of the Impreza squad in the mid-1990s, with team principal, David Richards.

have been extended if Carlos had not gradually fallen out with the Prodrive operation.

Despite his good nature, Carlos found it difficult to work with McRae, and to easily accept team order instructions, and, like many others, he found it difficult to work with hard-nosed tobacco company marketing staff. Accordingly, at the end of 1995 he left Prodrive, continuing his career first with Ford, then with Toyota, then again with Ford, and finally with Citroën.

Petter Solberg

Norwegian-born Petter had a meteoric rise into works

Although the Imprezas took first, second and third in the Catalunya (Spain) event of 1996, it was an event marred by controversy. For team political reasons, Subaru wanted local hero Carlo Sainz to win, which left Colin McRae less than pleased. Carlos doesn't look too pleased either in this servicing shot towards the end.

First seen in the Legacy Turbo of 1989, this is the 16-valve flat-4 turbocharged engine which, in modified form, powered so many winning Imprezas in the 1990s and 2000s.

rallying. In 1996 his first ever rally car was a Toyota Celica, he started his first World really (Sweden) in 1998, and in 1999 he joined M-Sport's team of works Ford Focus WRCs as 'the apprentice' behind Colin McRae.

In his second Focus drive – a run on the Kenyan classic which happened at very short notice – he finished fifth, and in the first half of 2000 had had fourth, fifth and sixth places in M-Sport Focuses. This was the point at which he, and his British co-driver Phil Mills, were persuaded to join Subaru, which happened in mid-season, and resulted in some unsavoury contract wrangles. Prodrive, however, persisted, and got its man (who was 26-years-old at the time) – who then stayed with the team for several more seasons.

Although he achieved little in an Impreza at first, his

Would Petter Solberg rather drive a rally car, or enjoy himself? Best not to ask ...

'Possum' Bourne was a real Subaru folk-hero, not only 'down under', but wherever his fans could see him behind the wheel of an Impreza rally car.

first podium placing was second in the Acropolis in 2001, with the first outright victory following in Great Britain at the end of 2002. Although Petter, the handsome, blond-haired Scandinavian soon got a reputation as something of a hell-raiser in his private life, who loved his parties and nights out, this never got in the way of his rallying.

Once he got the winning habit at Subaru, he was rarely satisfied with anything less than victory or, at the very least, a place in the top three. In his first five seasons he won the World Drivers' Championship in 2003, and was second in

2002, 2004 and 2005: it was only the fact that the Impreza was not quite as fast as the opposition from Citroën and Peugeot that stopped him from improving on that.

As he started his seventh season with Prodrive, he had already won twelve World rallies, and looked certain to add to that score in the future.

In a very busy season, Prodrive star Petter Solberg won no fewer than five World events in 2004 – that on the Rally GB being the fourth success. But he had to fight for it – his winning margin over Sebastian Loeb's Citroen was just six seconds.

Competition story

The Impreza's career

Before the 1990s, and the arrival of the four-wheel drive Legacy, Subaru had never been a credible force in World rallying. Earlier, less powerful models had appeared in the Safari, and in Far Eastern events, but had only been able to challenge where reliability, and not performance, was the key to success.

As already described in the 'Car and team' section, although the structure and much of the Impreza's 'chassis' was new, the turbocharged flat-4 engine and the four-wheel drive transmission were a logical evolution of those of the Legacy.

Launched into World rallying in 1990 (their first event was the Safari), the 300bhp Legacy Turbos were too bulky (but not too heavy) to beat Lancia's Delta Integrale and Toyota's Celica GT-4, and not even drivers like Markku Alen, Ari Vatanen and Colin McRae could overcome that at first. In 1993, with a brand-new and colourful sponsor – the 555 cigarette brand from British American Tobacco – the Legacy was finally ready to record a victory. In New Zealand, McRae gave the Legacy (and himself!) its first and only World Championship success. 555-liveried Legacies finished 1-2-3 (Vatanen, McRae, Bourne) in the Hong Kong Beijing rally, which did not hold World status, but was very important indeed in the Far East.

Three weeks later, the first works Impreza Turbo started its first event, the 1000 Lakes.

1993

In July there was a fascinating short-term sensation. No doubt frustrated by the Legacy's recent failure on the Acropolis rally (two cars started, one crashed and one broke its suspension), Fuji Heavy Industry's President Kawai announced that, even

Subaru's President Kawai said that he would not allow the Impreza Turbo to start rallying before the old Legacy had won a World Championshp Rally. With Colin McRae driving, this was finally achieved in the Rally of New Zealand of 1993.

First time out, in Finland in 1993, where Ari Vatanen so nearly achieved a major victory, but had to settle for second place.

though the Impreza had been homologated, he would not approve of it going into World rallying before the Legacy had won at least one round. Less than a month later Colin McRae's Legacy delivered that victory, and it was all smiles once again!

Although Ari Vatanen's Impreza so nearly won the car's first World event – 1000 Lakes in Finland – the Prodrive works team was disappointed that he could only take second place. In difficult conditions, after setting 15 fastest stage times, and 17 other podium placings, he was slowed by the constant misting up of the inside of the car when water from the intercooler spray somehow got into the cabin. Markku Alen crashed on the very first stage – and never again drove for Subaru.

The snowy conditions of the 1993 RAC rally were very familiar to Ari Vatanen, where L555 STE – a really effective 'publicity' number plate – achieved fifth overall.

The team only started one other event – Great Britain – where Ari Vatanen took fifth place, and was not quite competitive, though Colin McRae was quick until a stone punctured his water radiator. Even so, the combined effort of Legacies and Imprezas gave Subaru third place in the World Drivers' Championship.

1994

Now it was time for a full World team effort. Twice World Champion Carlos Sainz joined the team, with Colin McRae as his formidable partner. It was a year in which Imprezas contested all World rounds except the Safari, winning three times, and were narrowly pipped to the Makes Championship

Carlos Sainz's very first drive for the Subaru team came in Monte Carlo, in January 1994, where he took third place overall.

by Toyota. They were still not the fastest cars in the series either – that honour probably went to the Ford Escort RS Cosworth.

The cars looked the same as the 1993 models but now had a programmable hydraulic front differential, which was adjustable from the cockpit. More significantly, they had changed tyre suppliers from Michelin to Pirelli, a partnership which would remain for the next decade. Privately-entered Group N cars, too, proved to be consistent winners.

Although Carlos was not quite on the pace in Monte Carlo, he took third place, while Colin McRae crashed on snow that had seemingly been laid by vengeful spectators!

The first of many victory celebrations for Prodrive and the Impreza came in Greece in mid-1994, where Colin McRae and Derek Ringer showed just what a rugged car the new Impreza Turbo actually was.

Repeating his Legacy success of 1993, Colin McRae went back to New Zealand to do the same job in this Impreza Turbo.

In San Remo in October 1994, Carlos Sainz set many fastest times, but was finally pipped by Auriol's Toyota, and finished second.

Carlos struggled again in Portugal (McRae retired after an engine bay fire), and took second place on tarmac in Corsica, where he traded many fastest stage times with Auriol's Toyota Celica. Colin McRae crashed ...

The first outright victory came in Greece, where Sainz beat all other competitors, the strength and pace of the Impreza being matched by its preparation, and by an accomplished team effort. Poor McRae was excluded after a control infringement which was not of his making. Carlos then took a gritty second place in Argentina, setting most

Not only did Colin McRae win the RAC rally of 1994 in this Impreza Turbo, but this also confirmed that the Prodrive/Impreza team was now ready to win the World Championship, which it would do in the following year.

fastest stage times, but losing by six seconds. Once again, Didier Auriol was his principal rival. Once again, Colin McRae crashed ...

Colin redeemed himself with an outright victory in New Zealand (it was just a year since he had notched up his first ever World win there, and where the Legacy had ended

Tobacco sponsorship

The first time British enthusiasts saw a tobacco brand sponsoring a competition car was when Lotus became 'John Player Lotus' in 1968. Rothmans soon joined in on the circuits, and, in the early 1970s, Embassy sponsored some Ford Escort rally cars.

Based in Aylesbury, British American Tobacco (BAT) began supporting World rallying in 1979, placing its Rothmans brand on works Escorts. After moving on to Opel in 1982 and 1983, it then abandoned rallying for a time in favour of Porsche and sports car racing.

In the meantime, BAT had another tobacco brand, 555, which was marketed very strongly in Asia and the Far East. BAT used this brand to sponsor a major rally (Hong Kong-Beijing) in the 1980s, so when the Japanese concern, Subaru, joined the World rallying scene with the Imprezas, it made logical sense for 555 to link up.

It was no coincidence, of course, that David Richards of Prodrive, which gained the contract to run the works Subaru cars in World rallying, should enjoy the support of 555, for he had already had strong and successful links with the parent company, BAT, for more than ten years. Prodrive-prepared Legacy rally cars (as driven by Colin McRae and Richard Burns) used Rothmans livery in the British Championship, but the 555 brand was linked with the works Imprezas from their debut in 1993.

Although the Prodrive cars lost their very obvious 555 support from 1999 to 2001, they retained the same basic (and very distinctive) yellow-on-blue colour scheme throughout, and the 555 branding returned in 2002, though not on every event.

In the next few years, more and more countries banned the use of cigarette sponsorship in sport of any kind (though the TV transmission of races from countries that still allowed tobacco support made this a really messy enforcement problem ...), so, from 2003, there was once again no sign of 555 on the Imprezas.

its own works career) though Sainz's car broke its engine, and local hero 'Possum' Bourne crashed his car. Subaru then 'rested' McRae for a while, so only Sainz competed in Finland, where he had not competed since 1991 – the result, third place, was a remarkable achievement.

San Remo was the scene of another ding-dong battle between Sainz's Impreza and Auriol's Toyota, with Carlos setting most fastest stage times but finishing second, just 21 seconds off the pace: if his Impreza had not suffered from fuel starvation problems he would surely have won.

If a Hollywood scriptwriter had produced the scenario for the RAC Rally of Great Britain, he would not have been believed, for on this occasion it was Colin McRae who took the outright victory, while Carlos Sainz was on his way to a secure second place when he went off the road on the last day, in a Welsh forest. Prodrive, though, earned every headline which resulted, and went back to Banbury to claim an even bigger effort for 1995: it was going to be a sensational and controversial season.

How many different cars did Prodrive use during the 1994 season? We will never know, because a mere five registration numbers were swopped between different machines, seemingly with impunity. Each number – L555BAT, L555REP, L555SRT, L555STE and M555STE – had obvious promotional benefits to the tobacco firm sponsoring this effort, while the suffix letters were acronyms whose meaning was immediately obvious to most enthusiasts.

1995

Once again Prodrive relied on two world-class drivers

The start of a totally successful season for the Imprezas – Carlos Sainz, in L555 REP, on his way to winning the 1995 Monte Carlo rally – Subaru's first victory in this classic event.

– Carlos Sainz and Colin McRae – and once again it relied on the same very small fleet of 555-sponsored Imprezas for the season (theoretically at least!). History shows us that the team comfortably won the Makes Championship, and that Colin McRae won the Drivers' Championship. There was also the matter of five event victories (in eight World events), and a sometimes bitter rivalry between the proud Spaniard and the taciturn Scot.

During the season, many detail changes and improvements helped hone the cars (see 'Car and team') though peak power and torque were both slightly reduced because of newly applied turbocharger restrictions, where the restrictor diameter had been reduced from 38mm to 34mm. To balance this, there were advances in transmissions, engine controls and reliability.

With three outright victories, Carlos Sainz was 'Mr Consistency' as usual, while Colin McRae suffered one accident, one retirement, and took two outright victories: if this had been fiction, not even an inventive copy-writer could have wrung more sporting drama out of the situation.

You can't win them all! This was Sweden in 1995, when all three cars suffered engine failure due to blocked lubrication systems.

One of the Rally of Portugal's most famous jumps – this shows Carlos Sainz on his way to winning the 1995 event, and taking the Championship lead.

According to the registration numbers carried by the works cars, throughout the year Subaru used three of the same old Impreza WRCs as it had employed in 1993 and 1994, but no-one except the publicists ever believed that this was so. Subaru, no doubt, re-shelled or even completely renewed its cars as necessary – it was not until 1997, when tighter World Rally Car regulations firmly linked one chassis/VIN number to one bodyshell, that this charade was discontinued. You want proof? From using three identities in 1995, Prodrive jumped to using 16 cars in 1997 ...

Looking as purposeful as ever, though running without 555 identification to satisfy local advertising limitations, the three Imprezas dominated the Monte Carlo rally, with only Delecour's Ford Escort RS Cosworth and Kankkunen's Toyota Celica able to realistically challenge. Although Carlos Sainz was often visibly angry at the latest FIA edicts which drastically reduced the amount of servicing the cars could receive (drivers sometimes had to change their own wheels and tyres between special

New Zealand in 1995 and – guess what? – Colin McRae made it three Subaru victories in three years.

Spain 1995 where Colin McRae thought he should have won, but where team orders allowed Carlos Sainz to take the honours instead of him.

stages), he controlled his aggression and set up a faultless display.

Although Colin McRae led at first, he went off the road and Sainz took control to beat Delecour's hastily-prepared Escort by 145 seconds. Guest driver Piero Liatti of Italy (who would spend much of the season in Italian Championship rounds) finished well down in ninth place. Sainz, running at a controlled pace, set seven fastest times on the 21 stages; Colin McRae, on the other hand, was fiery – but crashed on the 12th stage.

As Carlos said afterwards: "To win this event you need a good car, good tyres and a good team – without all of these you cannot win ..." – and it was typical of this superstar that the driver's contribution was not mentioned. This, incidentally, was Subaru's first ever victory in the Monte Carlo rally.

Not only did Colin McRae win the 1995 RAC rally for the second year running, he also became World Rally Champion, with Subaru also winning the Manufacturers' series.

After such a dream start, three weeks later it all went wrong in Sweden. The Imprezas were fast, but not fast enough. Although they set fastest stage times, none of the cars ever led this snowbound event – and all three cars retired, not through crashes, you understand, but due to engine failures. Amazingly, all three suffered the same problem, which was not physically catastrophic, but was terminal – blocked oil pressure relief valves.

Order was restored on Portuguese gravel, Sainz winning the event by just 12 seconds from Juha Kankkunen's Toyota

New name, future World Champion – Richard Burns on his way to taking third place in the 1995 RAC rally. Overt tobacco sponsorship was forbidden on this event, hence the different 'non-555' colour scheme.

– with Colin McRae a further minute adrift and Richard Burns finishing seventh in the third of the team cars. But not even Sainz was perfect, for he crashed at one stage and damaged his car's brakes, but somehow kept going to the next service point.

Corsica – hot, dry, all-tarmac – was totally different from Portugal, yet the Imprezas were still competitive, with Sainz, McRae and Liatti taking 4-5-6 on an event that favoured tarmac-specialists like Auriol (Toyota) and Delecour (Ford Escort). Afterwards, team technicians were convinced that they could have gone better if their Pirelli tyres had been able to match the Michelin-shod opposition.

Down under in July, in New Zealand, Subaru was all smiles once again, for Colin McRae won the event, making it three McRae/Subaru successes in three years. Carlos Sainz did not start as he had suffered a shoulder injury following a mountain biking accident a month earlier), his place being taken by local hero 'Possum' Bourne, who finished seventh, while Richard Burns retired on the third day when his engine let go.

By mid-September, when the team tackled the Telstra Rally Australia, Sainz was fit again, though maybe not fit enough, for this was a long, hot, dusty event (based in Perth, Western Australia), where McRae set seven fastest times and 17 more podium placings, while Sainz was barely able to set fourth fastest.

World rallying was at its closest in this period and, after this event, both Manufacturers' and Drivers' Championship standings were finely balanced. With big personalities and big sponsors involved, this left Prodrive with a big challenge – both personally and for the sponsors – to be satisfied.

Matters came to a head in the all-tarmac Rally of Spain (Catalunya) where the pace-setting Toyota Celicas were suddenly disqualified from completing the event after doubts arose about the legality of their engines. (These doubts were later upheld by inspection, and the Toyota was disgraced, and banned from World rallying forthwith, until 1997.) This left the combination of the latest Impreza, the latest Pirelli tyres, superb preparation and three world-class drivers to dominate the event.

Once the Toyotas had been thrown out, victory was always going to go to one of two Impreza drivers – local hero Carlos Sainz or Colin McRae – but which one? Faced with a dilemma, team boss David Richards applied team orders – decreeing that whichever driver was ahead at the start of the last day should win the event. OK up to a point, but though Sainz led on that morning, McRae passed him during the day, and had to be forcefully told to slow down on the very last stage – which he did with ill grace. In the end, Carlos won the event by 51 seconds.

This meant that the two Impreza drivers started the RAC Rally of Great Britain with the same points score – and could fight it out without team orders getting in the way. With no works Toyotas on parade, and with Ford and Mitsubishi out of sorts, Subaru put on a brutal display of strength. Thriving on his home ground, with a mass of adoring fans urging him on, Colin McRae was fastest on 18 of the 28 special stages, and out of the top three only once! Sainz had to be satisfied with five fastest times and 15 second fastests, while Richard Burns ended up in third place.

It was a steamroller end to a steamroller season, with Subaru winning the Makes title, McRae the Drivers' title, and Sainz second, close behind him. The only cloud on the horizon was that Sainz had already told Subaru that he would be leaving the team – and although he was initially signed up for Toyota, when that team was thrown out of rallying he joined Ford for the next two seasons. Richard Burns, too, moved on, to try his hand in the Mitsubishi team.

1996

Following the soap opera dramas of 1995, another season, another derivative of the Impreza, and another series of high-profile performances followed in 1996. Although

Impreza – the most successful rally car of all time

At the end of 2005, the Impreza stood on the verge of becoming the most successful world-class rally car of all time. In thirteen seasons – 1993-2005 inclusive – Imprezas had won no fewer than 46 events, which put them exactly on a par with the Lancia Delta HF 4x4/Integrale family of 1987-92.

No other model of car even came close. By using several families of four-wheel drive Celica, Toyota recorded 30 wins, the Mitsubishi Lancer Evos had 28 victories, while the closely related Citroën Xsara WRC and Peugeot 206 WRC types each won 24 events. The pioneer of four-wheel drive rallying, Audi, won 23 events in the 1980s with Quattros and Sport Quattros.

In 2006, for sure, the Impreza looked certain to become the most successful rally car of all time. More than this, it had enjoyed a career of unparalleled consistency and success which no other marque looked likely to emulate for many years.

The new World Championship combination – Impreza Turbo + Colin McRae – flying very high in Sweden, on the narrowest-possible studded tyres. After three years, Subaru had begun to use different registration plates too – with Colin due to carry N1 WRC throughout the year.

Kenneth Eriksson's Impreza Turbo rushing past an unfamiliar backdrop – Kenya, Easter weekend, and the Safari rally of 1996, where he took a well-deserved second place.

Although McRae had previously won the Rally of Indonesia, that had been in years when it was not a World event. Best Impreza performance in 1996 was set by Piero Liatti, who finished second.

Back in the old routine – Colin McRae at his very best in a 'rough road' Impreza, amid stunning scenery on his way to winning the Acropolis rally of 1996. No-one could match his pace on that occasion.

Subaru realised that a new rallying formula – for World Rally Cars – would take effect in 1997, there was no let-up in development activity: with the glamorous, high-profile and forceful backing of British American Tobacco, a full effort was always likely.

With Carlos Sainz now driving for Ford, Colin McRae

Mud, mud, inglorious mud – watersplashes caused the Impreza Turbos big problems in Australia 1996, which hampered the team cars at times. The best finish was second place, recorded by Kenneth Eriksson though Colin McRae, harder hit by the water, took fourth only.

became de facto team leader, and Kenneth Eriksson was hired to back him. Although it was, in some ways, to be a quieter season, the Impreza would still notch up three outright wins (Colin McRae recorded all of them), and once again Subaru won the Makes' Championship, though McRae had to settle for second in the drivers' series. This, incidentally, was the start of the four-year Makinen/Mitsubishi dominance of World rallying, and Subaru's performances should all be measured against that statistic.

Although there wasn't much snow before the Swedish rally (some of the usual ploughed banks were conspicuously absent), a lot of it fell during the event, turning it into a classic battle. In a tight finish – only 88 seconds separated first from fourth – Colin McRae finished third, with Eriksson fifth: neither Didier Auriol nor Piero Liatti seemed to be as comfortable, for they preferred tarmac with sun on their backs.

For this, and every other event in his 1996 World Championship season (and if you believe this, you'll believe anything ...) McRae's Imprezas carried a new identity – N1 WRC – which every 'identity anorak' immediately realised meant 'No 1 Driver in the World Rally Championship'! Behind that identity, this 'one car' was crashed several times, rolled badly in Argentina, and was totally wrecked in Finland. So much for registration numbers ...

The team then dashed off to Thailand (a non-World event, but the opening round in the Asia-Pacific series, which was naturally dear to Subaru's heart). Although there was little top-class competition to the 555-liveried cars, they did well to finish 1-2-3, with McRae taking the honours in – guess what? – N1 WRC!

Competition on the Safari, of course, was much more intense, and although Subaru was not content with the result – the Imprezas suffered many suspension and shock absorber breakages caused by the rough and hot conditions – Eriksson took second place (11 minutes behind the winning Mitsubishi), with McRae fourth and Liatti fifth.

Driving yet another N1 WRC – that number followed to several brand new Prodrive Imprezas! – Colin McRae won the San Remo rally in October 1996.

There was more disappointment close to home on the Rally Indonesia (this was the first time the event had appeared in the World Championship), where Subaru had hoped to win. Both McRae and Eriksson crashed their Imprezas, while Liatti finished second to Sainz's Escort RS Cosworth – but a mere 23 seconds behind.

Three weeks later, though, McRae made up for all this by winning the Greek Acropolis rally – and also by beating his fiercest rival, Tommy Makinen (Mitsubishi). Although McRae led from start to finish, how close was the competition? Just look at the statistics – for the winning gap was only 50 seconds, and the two shared all but five fastest stage times. A new type of Pirelli tyre and sheer bloody-minded determination both helped. It was now obvious that although McRae occasionally tended to go over the limit and crash, he was always totally committed to winning, and would drag a mortally wounded car to the finish if that was at all possible. Not even a last-minute propeller shaft bearing failure could deny him this time!

Having then won in the Asia-Pacific rally of Malaysia, Kenneth Eriksson clearly loved the Argentina rally which followed, and finished a strong third (behind Makinen's Mitsubishi and Sainz's Ford). For Colin McRae, however, the whole event was a nightmare. First of all he hit a spectator on the first stage (who was actually standing in the road taking photographs), and then he hit a rock on the fourth stage. Having lost much time at service having the rear of the car re-built he then left in a great hurry, and was subsequently fined for speeding in a restricted area. Only two stages later he went off again, reducing his Impreza to a pile of scrap!

McRae, a very strong character with great fans and great detractors, was strongly criticised. Although well-used to such pressure, maybe he was badly affected by this escapade, for on the next event he tackled – the Finnish 1000 Lakes – he comprehensively wrote off yet another N1 WRC: it was the third time in the season that an accident had caused him to retire from an event. Team-mate Kenneth Eriksson could not match the leading times, so Subaru looked ahead for better things the following month, in Australia.

This time it was Eriksson's turn to finish second (guess what? – to Tommi Makinen's Mitsubishi), but McRae definitely looked subdued, and was out-driven by his team-mate, to take fourth place. By this time, too, it was clear that all was not well inside the McRae car, where he and co-driver Derek Ringer were no longer content with each other. After the event Subaru announced that Ringer would leave the team at the end of the year. Why? McRae would not say, while Ringer made it clear that he had been sacked against his will ...

By mid-October, and the San Remo rally, McRae had shrugged of the memory of a US $250,000 fine for his Argentinian escapade, and was back on form. Not even a pre-event brush with the Italian police for speeding on an autostrada could stop him. In a torrid, head-to-head battle with Carlos Sainz's Ford Escort RS Cosworth, each driver took five fastest stage times, and a similar number of minor placings. At the end of a four-day event, the two outpaced every other car, and finished just 22 seconds apart – with McRae winning: it helped, no doubt, that Makinen's Mitsubishi crashed on the very first stage!

One more World event remained in Subaru's 1996 programme – an event where McRae not only signalled that all was well in his head, but where the Prodrive team confirmed its lead over Mitsubishi, to lift the Makes Championship for the second consecutive year.

It was in Spain that McRae's progress was totally spellbinding. Not only did he win the event, with team-mate Piero Liatti second (by just seven seconds), but for Subaru this was all done without the shame of team orders hanging over them. In 1995, Colin had been ordered to slow down to allow Carlos Sainz to win his 'home' event, but on this occasion he had to battle to beat Liatti: in fact he did not take the lead until two stages from home.

And so it was that the four year career of the works Subaru Impreza 555 came to an end, but Subaru was not unhappy about that, as a new derivative of this successful car, the Impreza World Rally car, was on the way. Since mid-1993, works Impreza 555s had won two World Makes Championships, Colin McRae had won the Drivers' series in 1995, and the team had won no fewer than 11 individual

Celebrations all round in Spain in 1996, where Subaru confirmed its second consecutive World Manufacturers' Rally Championship.

events. It was an impressive record – but it was one which the World Rally car would totally obliterate in the next few years.

1997

For the first time ever (the World series had been set up as long ago as 1973), the FIA promoted a 14-event Championship, in which teams were required to compete in all events if they were to score points. Expensive! For 1997, and for Subaru, World rallying had changed considerably.

Group A motorsport was abandoned in favour of the new World Rally Car formula, which meant that the Impreza World Rally Car (described more fully in 'Car and Team') took over from the Impreza 555. Continuity, however, came

The World Rally Car made an impressive start to the 1997 season, not only winning in Monte Carlo but here, in Sweden also, with Kenneth Eriksson behind the wheel.

from the re-appointment of Prodrive to run the works rally team, and for Colin McRae, Kenneth Eriksson and Piero Liatti to be the top drivers.

Thus re-equipped, Subaru carried on, just as competitive, forceful, and crushingly successful as ever. In a 14-event World Championship, not only would the new Impreza win

Amazingly, on its very first appearance on the Safari, the new Impreza WRC won outright, with Colin McRae and co-driver Nicky Grist in the cabin. The rest of the massive Prodrive team, of course, was overjoyed by that success.

eight times, but Colin McRae took five of those victories, failing to beat Mitsubishi's Tommi Makinen to the Drivers' crown by just one point: if his year had been accident-free, he might have made it to the top step. Kenneth Eriksson won twice, and Piero Liatti once.

This was almost as good a start as Subaru could have wished, for it proved that all the basic thinking behind the new Impreza WRC was well-founded. The record showed that this car was a potential winner in all conditions – tarmac, gravel, hot, cold, wet, dry or wintry.

In Monte Carlo, Piero Liatti gave the team a great start to the year by winning from Carlos Sainz's Ford Escort WRC, though McRae crashed – twice. Sainz was even closer in Sweden, the margin being down to 16 seconds, and this

Pirelli loyalty – used on every works Impreza since 1993

From the day that the Impreza Turbo rally car was launched in 1993, to 2005/06, Subaru and Prodrive have stayed loyal to one tyre supplier – Pirelli. Other rival manufacturers have often changed suppliers, either because they forecast technical advantages, or there were good commercial reasons for doing so.

Pirelli, the Italian-based tyre supplier, had several British manufacturing plants for road vehicle tyres (but not motorsport tyres), and had always retained a strong motorsport operation. Even stronger when it was also supporting Italian manufacturers (such as Fiat or Lancia), Pirelli was always competitive in World rallying, though the records show that in some conditions, and at some periods, it was not perhaps as competitive as its biggest rival, Michelin.

Just as this book was being completed, Pirelli announced that it would pull out of World Championship rallying at the end of 2006, which partly explains why the Impreza WRC was no longer as competitive in the last few months of its works career.

---

time victory went to Eriksson on home snow, and Colin McRae suffered three time-consuming spins.

Fortunately, it all came right in Kenya, where Colin duly won his own first Safari (he was the very first British-based driver ever to do that, too), beating future rival Richard Burns by seven comfortable minutes, although it was not achieved without at least one high-speed crash. This time Eriksson's luck was out, for his WRC suffered suspension damage after hitting a large rock. Even so, that made it five World rally wins in succession ...

Lady Luck then deserted Subaru when both cars retired from the Rally of Portugal with engine problems caused by disintegrating camshaft pulleys, and three weeks later in Spain, Piero Liatti's WRC was denied victory (by Tommi Makinen) by just seven seconds, while Colin McRae's car suffered a puncture on a long stage which cost him some minutes. Amazingly, it all then came right again when Colin McRae's ex-Catalunya car produced a fine victory (by just eight seconds over Sainz's Ford) in Corsica: running on the very latest Pirelli tyres, and down to the minimum weight limit, this was Colin's, and Subaru's, first ever success on this tight little island.

Subaru then had to give best to Tommi Makinen's Mitsubishi in Argentina, where McRae finished second (hampered by some mechanical problems) and Kenneth Eriksson third, but both the Makes' and Drivers' championships were now hotting up nicely. If McRae had not punctured in Spain, and if Makinen had not crashed (after hitting an animal) in Corsica ...

Subaru's 1997 showing in Greece was a complete wipe-out (McRae had won in 1996) when McRae crashed and broke his steering, while Eriksson's car broke its steering and crashed badly – both cars were eliminated. Down under, in New Zealand, McRae's Impreza led comfortably for the first eight stages, before the engine abruptly stopped working: on the other hand, Eriksson's repaired ex-Acropolis car won the event – it was his sixth World success in a distinguished career.

Three weeks later in Finland, both Imprezas retired with sudden engine failure, both of them suffering from camshaft pulley breakages causing all drive to the camshafts to fail, and the engines stopped at once. Because this had happened several times earlier in the season, Prodrive and STI were greatly concerned, putting it down to an unexplained vibration problem which only cropped up on events, but never on the test-bed – this was eventually solved by a redesign.

On the other side of the world, in Indonesia, there was yet more sporting disaster for Subaru. Colin McRae led convincingly up to half-distance, then crashed into a tree: after recovery, with badly mangled bodywork, the WRC's

In San Remo in 1997, Colin McRae's Impreza World Rally Car won by only six seconds from his team-mate Piero Liatti. It needed real bravery to drive so quickly, close to so many rabid enthusiasts.

engine overheated and caught fire and was ruined. Kenneth Eriksson, on the other hand, could not keep up with the flying Ford Escorts.

Then, in the last three events of this 14-event Championship, Colin McRae finished with a real flourish, winning each of them. First of all, in San Remo, Subaru applied team orders so that the fastest Subaru driver, local hero Piero Liatti, dutifully dropped back to finish six seconds behind the star, though in Australia there was no need for any fudging. In that event the battle was between the Scot and Tommi Makinen's Mitsubishi, sharing many fastest and minor stage placings, the final gap being just six seconds once again!

Before the RAC Rally of Great Britain got started from

Determined to make up for the disappointments of 1996, Colin McRae/Nicky Grist won the Rally Australia – but by just six seconds from Tommi Makinen's Mitsubishi. No problems with water in the engine this time round.

World rallying could be a bit miserable at times – such as here, in the mud and fog of the British RAC rally. Not that Colin McRae let that get him down – he won the event for the third year, and Subaru won the World Championship for Makes yet again.

Cheltenham in November, Subaru had already landed the Makes Championship, but between McRae and Makinen it was still all to play for. For McRae to win his second title, Makinen would have to retire – and this he did not do. Driving like a man possessed over speed sections which were often very foggy, and in front of his adoring home fans,

McRae made no mistakes. Setting 15 fastest stage times (out of 26 stages in total), and fighting off a big challenge from Richard Burns' Mitsubishi, he eventually won his third RAC rally in four years (all of them in Imprezas), by nearly three minutes from Juha Kankkunen's Ford Escort. But it wasn't enough, for a rather subdued Makinen took sixth place, which deprived McRae of the Drivers' crown by a single point!

As far as Subaru was concerned, this had been a hugely expensive assault on a 14-event Championship, where it had used no fewer than 16 newly-constructed Impreza WRCs, but no 'face' had been lost, and the team looked forward to more success in 1998.

1998

For the new season, Prodrive made one important change to its driving line-up. Although Colin McRae stayed on board as team leader (though this would be his last season), it was the likeable Italian, Piero Liatti, who became his regular supporter, as Kenneth Eriksson drove only once (in Sweden)

After a difficult start to the 1998 season, which sapped his morale, Colin McRae bounced back to win the Rally of Portugal. By this time the Impreza WRC, if not its range of Pirelli tyres, was always capable of winning on any surface. Dustbath, anyone?

Colin McRae had won in Corsica in 1997, and now he did it all again in 1998, in one of his finest tarmac drives for the Prodrive team.

before moving off to lead the newly-founded European Hyundai operation. The Impreza WRC itself was visually little changed, though all manner of improvements were added out of sight (see 'Car and team'). Even so, the Impreza was by no means as successful in 1998 as it had been in 1997. Most other teams might have been satisfied with three

This Prodrive Impreza WRC is on its way to winning the Tour de Corse. The notice 'Interdit au Public' means 'No public allowed' – so who are all those enthusiastic spectators?

outright victories (all to McRae), but for Subaru, and by its previous standards, this was not good enough. Gradually, team morale slipped away (especially as British American Tobacco decided to end its long-running 555 sponsorship at the end of the season) – and it showed.

The first upset came in Monte Carlo, where the Imprezas

If you think that World rallying is glamorous, look carefully at this shot of Colin McRae on his way to winning the 1998 Acropolis – in searing hot temperatures, always choked by dust, and with the constant barrage of grit and stones underneath the skid shields ...

Although that was no way to start the year, Colin McRae then made up for it all by winning in Portugal – but by just 2.1 seconds, from Sainz's Toyota! Colin may have set the most fastest stage times, but rallying didn't get much tighter than that. Even so, it was a different story one rally – and one country – along. In Spain, the team's Pirelli tyres were simply not up to the pace of rival teams using Michelin, and the Imprezas were not competitive. Both works cars retired, Liatti's after hitting a bridge, and McRae's being withdrawn in disgust!

For McRae, though, the only way was up, and he duly delivered a victory on the twisty tarmac of Corsica, with Liatti in third place. At a stroke Subaru found itself back in the lead for the Makes Championship, and team morale was transformed.

Even so, Subaru's 1998 fortunes seemed to be on a perpetual see-saw. In Argentina, McRae set no fewer than 15 fastest times (of a total of 23 stages) – yet suffered one particularly harrowing incident in mid-stage, where he and co-driver Nicky Grist could not easily remove a damaged wheel because it was jammed up into the wheelarch; undaunted, they tried to drive on like that, until the wheel disintegrated, and they had to complete two more stages with damaged suspension! In the circumstances fifth place, just 78 seconds off the pace, was a remarkable achievement.

were not only slightly off the pace (McRae finished third, and Liatti fourth), but the event was won by Carlos Sainz's Toyota Corolla WRC, which was still new and virtually unproven. McRae blamed his Pirelli tyres for this failing, as most of the opposition was using Michelin, which seemed to have the best snow/ice equipment.

This was the story in snow-covered Sweden, where Kenneth Eriksson (in his only works Subaru drive of the year) finished fourth, and McRae eventually retired with engine electrical failure. Neither Impreza was on the pace, for neither driver ever recorded a top-two stage time, nor did their luck change on the dry and dusty Safari, where both works cars suffered overheating and broken engines.

Colin McRae took fourth place in Australia in 1998, his last ever finish in an Impreza, before he left the team at the end of the season. The Impreza, however, had many more successes still to record.

The see-saw season then continued, with McRae winning the Acropolis rally – his second Greek victory in three years – but was unable to match the pace of the Toyotas in New Zealand. The Scot's growing frustration was now evident, for in August he not only crashed out of the 1000 Lakes, but also announced his intention to join Ford (to drive the new-generation Focus) in 1999. Piero Liatti took second place in San Remo (McRae was third), then after leading the field in Australia, McRae's turbocharger blew just two stages from home, and cost him a victory.

Finally there was the Rally of Great Britain, where the major battle was between two Brits – McRae in the Impreza WRC, and Richard Burns in a Mitsubishi. No-one even tried to match their pace, and the lead changed several times

A great showing in Argentina 1999, where Juha Kankkunen recorded his first victory for Subaru and Prodrive, with team-mate Richard Burns just two seconds behind in second place. It was a great win for a rejuvenated team.

– until on stage 20 when yet another turbocharger-related engine problem caused McRae's Impreza to falter and fail. Retirement in this way was no way to end a spectacular six year career at Subaru.

1999

This was a year that began with major changes, not only to the car, but to the driving team and the sponsorship support. Colin McRae now left Subaru for Ford, and Richard Burns had jumped ship from Mitsubishi to join Subaru for 1999 and beyond, while Juha Kankkunen had moved over from Ford to replace Piero Liatti. Ex-Ford star Bruno Thiry joined the team for the first half of the season.

At the same time, Subaru had lost its tobacco

What an important victory this was for Richard Burns in the 1999 Rally of Argentina – it was his first ever in a World rally for Subaru. There would be many more in the future.

sponsorship from 555 at the end of the 1998 season. For the new season the Impreza had benefited from many detail revisions – which was enough for it to be re-homologated, and for all traces of 555 to disappear from the car's livery and from its entrant's name. Now totally financed from Japan, the Prodrive effort ran without a headline sponsor or an oil company contract: along with Seat, it was the only team to run on Pirelli tyres.

No wonder Juha Kankkunen looked so delighted after winning the 1999 Rally Finland for Subaru. His previous victory had been as long ago as 1993. The front of the Prodrive WRC looks tatty as it had suffered a lot of stone and grit blasting in the previous few days.

How did the team's fortune compare with 1998? Better, but not good enough, as Subaru lost out to Toyota in the Makes series by a mere four points, while Richard Burns had to give best to Tommi Makinen in the race for the Drivers' crown, although there would be five wins throughout the season – and the cars were always among the pace setters.

Even so, it was a season which started slowly, as the first win did not turn up until Argentina in May. Juha Kankkunen took second place in Monte Carlo, but could not catch the flying Fords or Mitsubishis, while in Sweden the team was simply off the pace, blaming the tyres for a lack of snow/ice performance. Then, on Safari, it got even worse, when

Richard Burns and his Impreza WRC, well sideways, and as committed as ever, on the way to winning the Rally of Great Britain in 1999. This was Richard's third win of the year, the Impreza's fifth – and the Impreza's fourth victory in Britain since 1994.

all three team cars retired from a hot and rough event: Richard Burns led the event before his suspension failed, but two other cars (Kankkunen and Thiry) stopped with obscure engine-related electronics failures.

In Portugal, at least, Burns finished, and in fourth place at that, only one minute behind McRae's winning Focus, though Kankkunen's engine failed near the finish. All three cars then finished Catalunya/Spain close together – in fifth/sixth/seventh – using fly-by-wire gearchange mechanisms for the first time, though these were still troublesome. Even so, good, brave but losing performances were not what Subaru's Japanese bosses expected or enjoyed. After Corsica, therefore, they must have been feeling murderous, for Richard Burns could only take seventh place, while Thiry crashed out, and Kankkunen (who hated tarmac rallying) did not even start: once again, and fairly or not, Pirelli took the blame.

Something, surely had to give, and in Argentina it duly did. With Prodrive opting to look after only two cars in future, the ill-fated Thiry left the team. On this gruelling loose-surface event, not only did Kankkunen win the event, but Burns followed him closely in second place: the gap was a mere 2.4 seconds, and Burns had led up until the penultimate special stage – team orders, Prodrive insisted, were not applied. Nor were they needed in Greece, where, in another astonishingly demanding event, Richard Burns won his first event for Subaru, while team-mate Kankkunen's effort was foiled when the rear suspension sub-frame broke up under the battering.

Disappointment followed in New Zealand, where Kankkunen's second place was not what he had expected, and Burn's car broke its transmission. But it all came good again for Prodrive in Finland (no longer called the 1000 Lakes ...) where Kankkunen won, Richard Burns took second place just ten seconds behind him, and only Marcus Gronholm (Peugeot 206 WRC) could begin to match their speed. It would, of course, have been wonderful if Subaru could then win the China Rally (which was included in the World Championship for the first time, and sponsored by 555 tobacco), but Burns and Kankkunen had to settle for second and fourth: tyre choice, it transpired, was all important here.

With three events to go, both Championships now seemed to be out of reach, so failure in San Remo (Kankkunen hated tarmac, and Burns' transmission broke) was not quite heartbreaking. In any case, Richard Burns' Imprezas then went on to win the final two events. In Australia, he fought mile-by-mile against Carlos Sainz's Toyota, though team-mate Kankkunen's car broke its suspension. Back home, in the Rally of Great Britain, it was a royal procession with one or other of the Imprezas leading from stage 2; Richard Burns won his second successful British event, and Juha took second place – this in spite of Burns' car suffering an engine bay fire in one service point after the oil filter bowl came loose!

Although Juha Kankkunen did not enjoy the Monte Carlo, with its constantly changing surfaces, he put in a consistent performance in 2000 to take third place.

In an astonishingly mature performance, Richard Burns won his second Safari rally in 2000 (his first had been in a Mitsubishi in 1998), ahead of team-mate Juha Kankkunen. The Prodrive Subarus were 100 per cent reliable in this hot, dusty and rocky event.

2000

This was another year of transition, with Prodrive completing the build of 20 '99 Model' WRCs, then building another 12 'WRC2000' types. The technical changes involved are detailed in 'Car and Team'. This was the season in which Peugeot's new 206WRC came on song, and in which the Ford Focus had more success. Although the Impreza was still very competitive, this was quite a mixed year, with Richard Burns winning four events, but with little support from team-mates: Subaru finished third in the Makes series, and Burns finished second in the Drivers' Championship,

Monte Carlo was a disappointment, when Burns' Subaru refused to start after a night-halt in the frigid open air, though Kankkunen's car finished third. So was Sweden, where Pirelli's tyres regularly shed studs (and grip), so a Burns-Kankkunen 1-2 in the Safari was a great relief, especially as Richard led throughout. Clearly Richard + Subaru WRC + rough roads was a winning combination,

Although Richard Burns won the Rally of Great Britain in 2000 – his third successive victory in the event – he had to cede the individual Drivers' Championship to rival Marcus Gronholm.

for they then triumphed again in Portugal and in Argentina. Along the way Burns took second place in the all-tarmac Catalunya/Spain, while Kankkunen took a strong third place behind Ford's Focus in the Acropolis.

Amazingly, both brand-new cars retired from the Rally of New Zealand with the same failing – cracked engine flywheels. There was another downer in Finland, where Richard Burns crashed his WRC immediately after the end of a stage! Cyprus (hot, dusty, rocky and slow – almost a clone of the Acropolis) was another disappointment for Burns (fourth after a bout of engine electronic problems) though he set several fastest stage times: by this stage in the season, Kankkunen was visibly no longer happy with his lot, and rarely figured in the fastest times: he left the team at the end of the year. From Corsica (September) Petter Solberg joined the team, and though he did not figure in the results for 2000 it was clear that here was a new (Norwegian) star in the making.

Burns, the team's star driver, was fourth in Corsica, but was outpaced by the French Peugeots. WRC2000's engine let go in San Remo after the car had been crashed, punctured the radiator and lost all its water. Nor could Richard quite make it in Australia, though third by a mere 8.2 seconds shows just how tight World rallying had become. With one event to go, therefore, this left neither Peugeot's Marcus Gronholm (59 points), nor Richard Burns (50) yet confirmed as World Champion.

Which left Britain's Network Q rally, where Burns was shooting for a hat trick – and he duly delivered! On a 17-stage/three-day event, Richard set five fastest times, and seven other 'podium' times, which was good enough to beat Colin McRae's Focus (which crashed) and Gronholm (who finished second, just 66 seconds behind him). What a season!

2001

Was this a season in which Prodrive changed too many things, so that it was not as competitive as usual? According to some statistics it looked like that. Or was it plain unlucky? Although Richard Burns won the World Drivers' Championship, the Impreza itself slumped to fourth in the Makes standings, and there was only one outright victory (for Burns in New Zealand) to celebrate. New drivers (too many drivers, at times?) perhaps? A new car with too many innovations? Or maybe it was just one of those years when the opposition – Peugeot and Ford in particular – make great advances.

Although Prodrive dabbled with entering four cars at times, Burns was the acknowledged team leader, with Petter Solberg and Markko Martin the 'coming-men' for the future. Prodrive, at least, made a clean break with the past, for it sold off all the old 2000 models, and started the season with the ugly new four-door car (see 'Car and Team').

All three team cars retired from Monte Carlo, while Richard Burns set many fastest times in Sweden, but spent

Richard Burns staged another great and gritty performance with his Impreza World Rally Car in Cyprus 2001, finishing second, just 16 seconds away from an outright win.

Petter Solberg of Norway finally recorded a great result for Subaru – second place in the 2001 Acropolis – and would eventually go on to become World Rally Champion.

Although Richard Burns won only one rally during the 2001 season, he was 'Mr Consistency' and would become World Champion. Here he is charging through a water-splash in Argentina, where he took second place.

There are some days – like this one for Richard Burns on Safari in 2001 – when you wish you'd stayed in bed. A catastrophic front suspension failure put him out of the running at a very early stage.

13 minutes (an age, in rallying terms) off the road in a snowdrift. Three of four Prodrive cars retired in Portugal, with Burns off the pace, and, in Spain, Burns was down in seventh place without a fastest time to his name. Things improved in Argentina (the Impreza was always a better 'gravel' car than a 'tarmac' machine), where Burns finished second after fighting stage-against-stage with Colin McRae's Ford Focus: Petter Solberg finished fifth, and showed real promise. Cyprus (also hot, dusty and rough) was a repeat performance, with Burns again second (by a mere 16 seconds), though Solberg's car retired after a fire, which gutted his new Impreza.

On the Acropolis, Colin McRae's Ford won yet again, with an Impreza second yet again (this time it was Petter

Solberg), though Burns' car broke its propeller shaft, and Arai's team car was consumed by fire. The Safari, held in July for the first time, should have been tailor-made for the Impreza, yet all three cars retired, all of them with suspension-related failures.

For Prodrive, whose self-imposed high standards required regular victories, was now in despair, for although Burns notched up another second place (by 25 seconds to Gronholm's Peugeot, so near and yet so far ...), his team-mates could not match his pace, and consistency. Richard did manage to win the Rally of New Zealand, while team-mate Solberg set the same number of fastest stage times (six out of 24). And this was the high point. Burns crashed out of San Remo on the very first stage (he mis-heard an instruction from his co-driver). While finishing fourth in Corsica he couldn't match the sheer speed of the Peugeot 206WRCs: team-mate Petter Solberg finished fifth, just one second behind him, and Markko Martin was sixth – so there was finally consistency, if not rally-winning pace. For Burns in Australia, yet another second place followed (how frustrating his year much have been), and his amazing consistency throughout the season saw him go into the last event of the season, the Rally of Great Britain, with every chance of winning the World Championship.

As the cars lined up in Cardiff, Colin McRae led Richard Burns by two points, and immediately sprang into a lead that seemed certain to clinch everything. Suddenly, almost inevitably, the Scot crashed his Focus, leaving Burns knowing that he need finish only fourth or higher to win the crown. In the event he paced himself superbly, did not take a single fastest stage time, and finished a serene third, behind the victorious Peugeots. Team-mate Solberg suffered from a mis-reading fuel refilling rig and ran out of fuel, while Markko Martin's engine let go. It was enough, though, and Subaru had yet another title to shout about, and looked ahead to making yet another fresh start in 2002.

2002

Because technical chief Christian Loriaux had left Prodrive in November 2001 (he moved north to work alongside

Maybe you can't win them all, but with yet another fine second placing in the Rally Finland of 2001, Richard Burns moved one step closer to the World Drivers' Championship.

On his way to victory in New Zealand 2001 (which made it five Subaru successes in nine years), Richard Burns climbed even further up the Drivers' Championship standings.

Malcolm Wilson on the Ford Focus WRC cars), it was, indeed, necessary to make a new start. New World Champion, Richard Burns, frustrated by his stop-go 2001 season, had defected to Peugeot for a new two-year contract, Markko Martin had defected to Ford, and Prodrive had learned its lesson about running four-car teams – it was

Underneath the floodlights of the 'Superspecial' stage in Perth on Rally Australia 2001, Richard Burns was on his way to yet another second place overall – his fourth of the year.

too much aggravation. The fresh-start, therefore, not only meant welcoming British American Tobacco's 555 cigarette brand back on to the cars, but having Petter Solberg (known as 'Mr Hollywood' for his nightclubbing reputation) joined by four-time World Champion Tommi Makinen. Would this be the kick-start that was needed?

In the previous month, Burns had been involved in a seedy contract dispute between Subaru (which wanted to retain him) and Peugeot (which wanted to hire him): though details were never released, it is thought that Peugeot had to pay a lot of money to buy out the option that Subaru had on his services!

All this high-profile manoeuvring caused more heat than light, as the latest version of the Impreza would only finish third in the Makes Championship. Makinen's record was poor, and even the glamorous young Solberg could only notch up one outright victory – at the very end of the year. Unhappily for Subaru, there were to be only two victories in what was a fraught season.

Even so, in Monte Carlo it all started well when Tommi Makinen won his debut event for Subaru, and Solberg (sixth, after problems) set five fastest stage times. Both cars retired

Petter Solberg carried a permanent competition number – 11 – throughout 2002, and his Impreza WRC was usually battling for the lead. Here, in San Remo, he took yet another third place.

in Sweden (one with a blocked radiator causing engine overheating, the other with engine piston failure, Makinen wrote off his brand-new car in Corsica, while Solberg's suffered punctures, and, in Spain, Makinen suffered an engine failure which followed a radiator-damaging crash.

The Imprezas faired better in Cyprus – third for Makinen, fifth for Solberg – though if Petter's throttle control had not failed on an early stage he might have won: fifth, and 2min 18sec off the pace was no reward. Makinen then comprehensively wrote off yet another Impreza in Argentina, while Solberg should have won, yet went off the road before ending up second, just four seconds behind Carlos Sainz's Ford Focus.

There was no let-up in Greece, where Makinen's car lost its power-steering, its brakes and a wheel (after an accident) in that order, while Solberg's Impreza was fast, but had a temperamental engine. The Impreza, which had already won two Safaris, should have made it three in July, but Makinen's car broke its suspension, and Solberg's turbocharger failed. Way off the pace in Finland, Solberg nevertheless took third place on sheer consistency, with Makinen sixth.

Subaru ran four Imprezas in Germany, but two crashed, one blew its gearbox, and only Makinen (sixth, and struggling) made it to the end. By this time Makinen was really out of sorts with his new team, as his transmission broke a drive shaft in San Remo, though Solberg recorded another third place. Not even in New Zealand (where Richard Burns had won in 2001) could the Imprezas win again, for Solberg's car broke its engine, and Makinen trailed home in third place.

Almost a completely new start for 2002 – new drivers, a modified car, and the return of '555' tobacco as main sponsors. Four-times World Champion Tommi Makinen joined the team, and began by winning the Monte Carlo rally.

No wonder Prodrive always carried replacement front bumper mouldings in its service/repair kits on rallies! Petter Solberg jumping high, then nose-diving, in Australia in 2002 – on his way to third.

In Australia, Makinen was excluded at the end of the event when his car was found to be underweight (it was running without a spare wheel at the time), while Solberg took third place, competitive again, and smiling for a change. The sun finally came out for Prodrive on the last event of the year – the Rally of Great Britain – where Solberg

Victory at last for Petter Solberg – his very first World victory, and in an Impreza WRC, too. Petter ('Mr Hollywood') waves an almighty trophy, and co-driver Philip Mills hides his face from the cameras.

was Solberg's (and his co-driver Phil Mills') very first World victory – and it would not be the last!

2003

After two rather fallow seasons, things looked up in 2003. Not only did Prodrive have another new (re-engineered) version of the Impreza, but it kept a settled driving team – Petter Solberg and Tommi Makinen continued from 2002. Even so, although team entries were still made by the 555 Subaru World Rally Team, there was no longer any evidence of '555' on the cars' livery.

The latest Impreza WRC was more successful, and more reliable. Petter Solberg won no fewer than four events outright, and also won the World Drivers' Championship. The team itself clawed its way up to a respectable third place in the Makes' Championship (no team could catch the flying Citroëns and Peugeots), and there were fewer silly breakdowns than before. All in all, this convinced the rallying world that the Impreza (which was now about to complete ten years at the top) was still ultra-competitive.

Nevertheless, in Monte Carlo the season started badly for Subaru, when both brand-new cars ended up off the road. Whoops! Second place for Makinen in Sweden was more encouraging, as was third for Solberg in New Zealand, though Turkey was a disappointment. Not even in Argentina (where Imprezas had won twice in recent years) could Solberg finish higher than fifth. Third and fifth in the Acropolis was, at least, more encouraging, but morale was now sagging badly.

It all came right for the Impreza, and for Petter Solberg, in Cyprus. Competitive from the start, and in the lead from the second morning, his Impreza set seven fastest stage times, and at the end he won the rally more than four minutes (an age in modern rally terms) ahead of the next man. For Makinen, though, there was more disappointment, and it

and Ford's Markko Martin fought head-to-head throughout, though Tommi Makinen could only take fourth place. Not only did Solberg set the most fastest times – eight of the 17 stages – but he looked supremely confident, and gloriously happy at the end of what had been a frustrating season. It

Carrying No. 8 for 2003, Tommi Makinen pushed himself to every limit, including this totally committed drive to second place in Sweden. Compared with 2002, there had been many visual and technical changes.

was clear that he and the Impreza were not totally suited to each other. For the rest of the season he never looked like winning: the balance of the campaign, no question, belonged to Solberg instead, and Makinen retired from the sport at the end of the season.

The success did not continue on the military tarmac roads of Germany, though, where Solberg was not well throughout, and where Pirelli's tarmac tyres didn't match up to those of Michelin (used by every other works team). Competitive once again in Finland, Solberg then took second place, after a long battle with Richard Burns' Peugeot – though he couldn't catch Markko Martin's Ford Focus. He then notched up a splendid victory in Australia, just 26 seconds ahead of Loeb's Citroën. This was Solberg at his best, battling to record nine fastest stage times, and never finishing slower than fourth.

On San Remo's tarmac stages, the Imprezas were once again outpaced by Michelin-clad cars, and to add insult to an unhappy weekend, Solberg's car ran out of fuel on a road section. Somehow, two weeks later, Subaru, Pirelli and Solberg regrouped to tackle the all-tarmac Corsica and, amazingly, claimed victory by 36 seconds from Sainz's Citroën – all this even though Solberg had crashed his brand-new car in pre-rally testing, forcing Prodrive's mechanics to carry out a back-breaking all-nighter to get it straightened out in time. It was typical of Prodrive's self-imposed standards, however, that when Solberg started the event, the car looked brand new ...

Not even Petter could then repeat the feat in Spain/Catalunya (where he took fifth place and recorded just two fastest stage times), but it all came to a glorious head in the Wales Rally GB in November. In the run-up to the event, the media made much of the fact that four drivers – Solberg, Sainz, Loeb and Richard Burns – could all still win the Drivers' Championship, and a battle royal was a prospect.

Burns had to withdraw when he collapsed the day before the start (tragically, although had already signed to return to Subaru in 2004, he would never drive again, and died in 2005), so this was a three-cornered battle, which became a head-to-head when Sainz crashed on the second stage, distracted by a burning smell inside his Citroën. On an 18-stage rally, thereafter, Solberg's Impreza was dominant,

Looks lonely, right? Even so, Petter Solberg was on his way to winning the Cyprus rally of 2003 – his first of four victories in the season.

This fine shot of Petter Solberg's car on the 2003 Tour de Corse shows just how hard the Impreza World Rally Car's suspension was on tarmac events. Petter won this event, his third of four outright victories in the season.

setting 13 fastest times and five second fastests. No other car/driver combination, surely, could have made such an impression.

2004

With the Impreza continuing into its 11th year (the World Rally Car derivative was starting its eighth year), Prodrive's

Twice a winning combination in 2003: Petter Solberg, Phil Mills and their Impreza World Rally Car S600 WRT on their way to victory in the 2003 Rally of Great Britain. Petter won four rounds in 2003, and became World Rally Champion.

main change was to re-shuffle the driving line-up. Naturally, newly-crowned World Drivers' Champion Petter Solberg remained as team leader, and for 2004 he was joined by 23-year-old Mikko Hirvonen of Finland, who had spent the previous season driving a privately-financed Ford Focus WRC, and brought external sponsorship with him. Mikko made a very tentative start to his works career, for he only finished fourth on two occasions, fifth on two others, and lower down in other events.

Yet again Subaru would finish third in the World Makes Championship (no-one, it seemed, could match Citroën's Xsara and Ford's rejuvenated Focus), and although Petter won no fewer than five events outright, this was still not quite enough, as he had to settle for second in the Drivers' Championship. Once again, this was an extremely crowded season, with no fewer than 15 events to be run between January and November: to score points in the Makes series, the works Imprezas were obliged to tackle all of them.

Petter Solberg's season was good – and bad – in parts, with five victories and three accidents – but he was always

Victory in New Zealand for Subaru and Petter Solberg in 2004 – Petter's first of five in this eventful season.

Petter and Subaru's second victory of the 2004 season came in June, in the heat, stones and all-pervasive dust of the Acropolis rally.

competitive, and always trying very hard. Unable to match Citroën and Ford times in Monte Carlo, and surprisingly subdued in Sweden too, he ought to have won in Mexico had electronic problems not led to a control infringement penalty.

Everything came right in New Zealand, where Petter narrowly beat Marcus Gronholm's Peugeot 307, though his fast run in Cyprus was hampered by engine overheating problems on the first day. Three weeks later, and after shifting across the Mediterranean to Greece, he then won the Acropolis, this time having to beat off Loeb's Citroën. Third in Turkey with a damaged car, retirement in Argentina after his engine swallowed much water after a river crossing incident, and retirement in Finland after wrecking his suspension in a high-speed accident all indicate what an up-and-down season it was for the 555 Subaru team.

In Germany, Petter wrote off his Impreza in an accident which probably outdid anything ever achieved by Colin McRae – he hit a concrete block, cartwheeled and comprehensively wrote off the machine – though he

Petter Solberg jumping high, long and very fast on his way to winning the World Rally of Sardinia in 2004 – it was his fifth of the season – and he would be runner-up in the Drivers' Championship.

bounced back at once to win the Rally of Japan (with a different car!), which mightily pleased Subaru. Notching up his third successive Rally GB victory was then an enormous pleasure (though it was only by six seconds from Loeb's Citroën), and he then made it three events on the run (for himself and Subaru) by once again beating Loeb, this time on the twisty tarmac roads of Sardinia.

The final three events of the season resulted in fifth in Corsica and in Spain/Catalunya, and a downbeat end to the year when he crashed his Impreza on a very early special stage.

2005

Another season, another round-the-world grind – for the World Rally Championship was getting evermore arduous. In 2005, there were no fewer than 16 qualifying rounds, all of which had to be entered for a manufacturer to score Championship points. Events spanned the globe – from Britain to Australia, from Argentina to Japan, and from Finland to Mexico. It was no wonder that, at the end of the year, both Prodrive and its star driver, Petter Solberg, deserved a good rest. In 2005, Chris Atkinson of Australia, and Stephene Sarrazin of France, joined Prodrive as Solberg's support drivers, though neither ever figured strongly. Atkinson's two best results, in fact, were third in Japan, and fourth in his native Australia. Sarrazin took fourth in Corsica, and eighth in Germany – both tarmac events. In many ways, for both driver and team, this was almost a repeat of the previous season, for Solberg's Imprezas marked up three outright victories, the team finished fourth in the Makes series

It's always good to win at home! On the World Rally Championship's first visit to Japan, Petter Solberg's works Impreza WRC won the event. Petter looks suitably relieved to mark up that first 'home win' ...

In 2005 the Impreza WRC recorded three outright victories – all of them to Petter Solberg's credit – the first being in Sweden, where Petter was well over two minutes ahead of the field after a total of 20 special stages. Ultra-narrow wheels and studded tyres are needed to get the best grip on this snowy event.

Local support in Cyprus 2005, but no success this time for Petter Solberg.

– and yet again it was the Loeb/Citroën combination that dominated the rallying scene.

Although Petter always gave his all, the Impreza was neither nimble enough, nor modern enough in its engineering, to beat the free-spending Citroën team on a regular basis. As ever, Pirelli supplied Prodrive's tyres, and if they seemed to be more competitive than before, they still had a difficult battle against Michelin.

Having crashed out of the Monte Carlo, Petter then won the next two events – Sweden by three minutes, and Mexico (in the revised-for-2005 Impreza) by 36 seconds, both from works Peugeot 307s. After that, what may come to be known as the 'Loeb avalanche' – six outright wins in succession – made all thoughts of a World Championship chase out of the question.

Neither Petter nor the Impreza, though, ever gave in. Third in New Zealand and second in Corsica were plucky performance, then his engine let go in Cyprus after it swallowed too much dirt, before once again finishing second in Turkey. Off the pace in Greece (where his car, in any case, was found to be underweight), he recovered to take third in Argentina, then fourth in Finland, before sagging

Peter Solberg and the Impreza WRC just love to go rallying in Britain – in 2005 they won their fourth consecutive British event, making it seven Impreza WRC victories in nine years.

Bad luck Petter – having set the most fastest stage times in Japan 2005, and led the event until two stages from home, he then hit a rock which had landed in the road, damaged his Impreza's steering, and was forced to retire.

badly to seventh in Germany (after the 2004 accident, he hated the military roads used for stages).

Suddenly, in Wales for the Rally of Great Britain, it all came right again – but not in the way he wanted it, for this was the event where Michael Park tragically lost his life when his driver, Markko Martin, lost control of his Peugeot and hit a tree in a high-speed accident. Never in the lead (he could not keep up with Loeb and Duval's Citroëns), Petter was gifted victory when Sebastien Loeb decided that he had no stomach for further competition on this event.

The professional show, however, had to go on. In the last four events of the season, Petter retired in Japan when leading (due to deranged steering after hitting a rock), managed fourth place in Corsica (without even setting

Having been off the road, and damaging the front end, Chris Atkinson's Impreza WRC needed a lot of attention before it could get going again. Even so, Atkinson recovered, to finish fourth, one of his best results of the season.

This classic study of Petter Solberg's Prodrive Impreza WRC diving deep in an Australian water-splash in 2005, sums up the rugged way that the Impreza had stayed at the top of World rallying for more than twelve years.

a fastest stage time!), could manage only 13th in Spain/Catalunya after he had crashed on the first day, while in Australia, he retired after leading the event, but (of all things) hit a kangaroo, killing the unfortunate animal and ruining the Impreza's cooling systems.

So it was that the Impreza came to the end of its 13th year in World rallying. By that time it had recorded no fewer than 46 outright victories, better than any other family of rally cars, and equalled at that moment by the front-engined/four-wheel drive pedigree of Lancia Delta 4x4/Integrales. One more victory in 2006 – and there seemed to be every reason for that to follow – would put it at the very pinnacle of rallying.

The Impreza's successor

At the time of writing, the Impreza World Rally Car's career was still not over. In 2005 (particularly with Petter Solberg behind the wheel) it was still competitive, and still a rally winner. Although Subaru was known to be developing a successor to the second-generation Impreza, by the beginning of 2006 it had not yet broken cover.

One thing, though, seems to be certain – that the combination of Subaru's engineering and four-wheel drive expertise, with the experience and sheer rally know-how of a team like Prodrive should be enough to keep the cars at the top of the results sheets for years to come.

Visit Veloce on the web – www.veloce.co.uk
Details of all books in print • Special offers • New book news • Gift vouchers

Works rally cars – World Championship rallies (and when first used)

Note: from 1993 to 1996, the same 'publicity' registration numbers appeared on several different cars, so definite identities they are virtually useless.

As examples, although they were legally acquired numbers, Subaru had been careful to acquire 'BAT', which stood for British American Tobacco, while 'SRT' stood for Subaru Rally Team, and 'STE' for Subaru Tecnica Europe. The following, however, is the list of when different identities first appeared – there being no 'new' cars in 1995,

1993
L555 BAT
L555 STE

1994
L555 REP
L555 SRT
M555 STE

1996
N1 WRC
L555 SRT
N555 BAT
N555 WRC

Starting in 1997, all Subarus were the much-revised World Rally Car types.

1997
P2 WRC
P3 WRC
P4 WRC
P6 WRC
P7 WRC
P8 WRC
P9 WRC
P10 WRC
P11 WRC
P12 WRC
P14 WRC
P16 WRC
P17 WRC
P18 WRC
P19 WRC
P982 YWL

1998
R7 WRC
R8 WRC
R9 WRC
R10 WRC
R11 WRC
R12 WRC
R14 WRC
R15 WRC
R16 WRC
R17 WRC
R19 WRC
R20 WRC
R30 WRC

1999
S6 SRT
S7 SRT
S8 SRT
S9 SRT
S10 SRT
T11 SRT
T11 SRT
T12 SRT
T14 SRT
T15 SRT

2000
T16 SRT
W17 SRT
W18 SRT
W19 SRT
W20 SRT
W21 SRT
W22 SRT
W23 SRT
W24 SRT
W25 SRT

2001
X1 SRT
X2 SRT
X3 SRT
X4 SRT
X5 SRT
X6 SRT
X7 SRT
X8 SRT
X9 SRT
X10 SRT
X11 SRT
X12 SRT
X14 SRT
X15 SRT
X16 SRT
X17 SRT
X19 SRT
X20 SRT
X21 SRT

2002
X23 SRT
X24 SRT
X26 SRT
X27 SRT
X28 SRT
PR02 SRT
PS02 SRT
PS02 SSS
PT02 SRT
TM02 SRT
TMO2 SSS

2003
S30 WRT
S40 WRT
S50 WRT
S60 WRT
S70 WRT
S80 WRT
S90 WRT
S100 WRT

S200 WRT
S300 WRT
S400 WRT
S500 WRT
S600 WRT
S700 WRT

2004
555 WRC
S800 WRT
AT53 SRT
CT53 SRT
JT53 SRT
LT53 SRT
MT53 SRT
NT53 SRT
OT53 SRT

RT53 SRT
ST53 SRT
YT53 SRT

2005
WT53 SRT
OU04 XNZ
AC54 WRC
BC54 WRC
CC54 WRC
EC54 WRC
GC54 WRC
HC54 WRC
JC54 WRC
LC54 WRC
MC54 WRC
NC54 WRC

Visit Veloce on the web – **www.veloce.co.uk**
Details of all books in print • Special offers • New book news • Gift vouchers

World and major European rally wins

Note: Impreza 555 from 1994 – 1996, Impreza WRC from 1997.

Event	Car	Drivers
1994		
Acropolis	L555 REP	Sainz/Moya
New Zealand	L555 BAT	McRae/Ringer
RAC	L555 BAT	McRae/Ringe
1995		
Monte Carlo	L555 REP	Sainz/Moya
Portugal	L555 REP	Sainz/Moya
New Zealand	L555 BAT	McRae/Ringer
Spain	L555 REP	Sainz/Moya
RAC	L555 BAT	McRae/Ringer
1996		
Acropolis	N1 WRC	McRae/Ringer
San Remo	N1 WRC	McRae/Ringer
Spain	N1 WRC	McRae/Ringer
1997		
Monte Carlo	P3 WRC	Liatti/Pons
Sweden	P5 WRC	Eriksson/Parmander
Safari	P8 WRC	McRae/Grist
Tour de Corse	P9 WRC	McRae/Grist
New Zealand	P11 WRC	Eriksson/Parmander
San Remo	P7 WRC	McRae/Grist
Australia	R18 WRC	McRae/Grist
RAC	P12 WRC	McRae/grist
1998		
Portugal	R19 WRC	McRae/Grist
Tour de Corse	R11 WRC	McRae/Grist
Acropolis	R11 WRC	McRae/Grist
1999		
Argentina	S8 SRT	Kankkunen/Repo
Acropolis	T12 SRT	Burns/Reid
1000 Lakes/Neste	T11 SRT	Kankkunen/Repo
Australia	T12 SRT	Burns/Reid
RAC	T14 SRT	Burns/Reid
2000		
Safari	T14 SRT	Burns/Reid
Portugal	W18 SRT	Burns/Reid
Argentina	W18 SRT	Burns/Reid
Great Britain	W25 SRT	Burns/Reid
2001		
New Zealand	X7 SRT	Burns/Reid
2002		
Monte Carlo	X28 SRT	Makinen/Lindstrom
Great Britain	X9 SRT	Solberg/Mills

Event	Car	Drivers
2003		
Cyprus	S80 WRT	Solberg/Mills
Australia	S600 WRT	Solberg/Mills
Tour de Corse	S700 WRT	Solberg/Mills
Great Britain	S600 WRT	Solberg/Mills
2004		
New Zealand	555 WRC	Solberg/Mills
Acropolis	JT53 SRT	Solberg/Mills
Japan	555 WRC	Solberg/Mills
GB	NT53 SRT	Solberg/Mills
Sardinia	MT53 SRT	Solberg/Mills
2005		
Sweden	WT53 SRT	Solberg/Mills
Mexico	AC54 WRC	Solberg/Mills
GB	LC54 WRC	Solberg/Mills

Index

Note: there are so many individual mentions of Prodrive, and of the Impreza, and all its derivatives, that no attempt has been made to index them.

555 cigarette sponsorship 9, 13, 29, 30, 38, 52, 59, 83, 100, 101, 103, 110

Andersson, Ove 10
Asia-Pacific Rally Championship 40
Audi (and models) 11, 37, 66
Auriol, Didier 15, 57-59, 65, 71

BAR F1 team 38, 40
Benetton F1 team 38
BMW (and models) 38, 39
British American Tobacco 9, 38, 39, 52, 59, 70, 83, 100
British Rally Championship 11, 40, 43
Burns, Richard 105, 106

Citroën (and models) 23, 44, 48, 50, 66, 103, 105, 107-110, 113, 116

David Richards Autosports 38, 39
Datsun (and models) 10
Delecour, Francois 62, 63, 65
Duval, Francois 116

Embassy tobacco sponsorship 59

Ferrari (and models) 38, 40
Fiat (and models) 77 (21/6)
Ford (and models) 9, 11, 13-17, 19, 20, 21, 23, 29, 37-40, 42, 44, 46, 48, 55, 59, 62, 63, 65, 66, 71, 73, 76-78, 81, 85, 86, 88, 91-93, 96-99, 101, 103, 105, 108, 109
Fuji Heavy Industries 15, 16, 37, 52

Gronholm, Marcus 89, 92, 93, 97, 109

Holmes, Martin 40
Honda (and models) 11
Hyundai (and models) 82

Jeep 12
Jensen 12
Jowett (and models) 17, 18

Kankkunen, Juha 62, 65, 81
Katsurada, Masaru 38
Kawai, President 52
Kuze, Yuichiro 39, 42

Lancia (and models) 9, 11, 13-16, 37, 40, 46, 52, 66, 77, 116
Land Rover 12
Lapworth, David 26, 28-30, 38, 40
Loeb, Sebastian 44, 50, 105, 109, 110, 113, 116
Loriaux, Christian 30, 40, 98
Lotus (and models) 59
Lucas-Girling test track 38

Makinen, Tommi 71, 73, 76-81
Martin, Markko 103, 105, 116
Mazda (and models) 12
McRae, Alister 42
McRae, Colin 96, 97
McRae, Jimmy 42
MG-Rover (and models) 34
Mitsubishi (and models) 9, 10, 12-14, 40, 44, 66, 71, 73, 76-79, 81, 85, 86, 88

Nissan (and models) 10, 14, 20

O'Dell, Des 40

Opel (and models) 59

Park, Michael 115
Peugeot (and models) 11, 23, 40, 41, 66, 89, 91, 93, 97, 99, 100, 103, 105, 109, 113, 116
Pond, Tony 39
Porsche (and models) 17, 18, 38, 39, 59
Porsche, Dr Ferdinand 17

Rallies:
- Acropolis (Greece) 10, 11, 49, 52, 56, 70, 73, 77, 84, 85, 89, 92, 95, 97, 101, 103, 109, 115
- Argentina 31, 57, 71, 73, 77, 84, 86-89, 92, 95, 96, 101, 103, 110, 115
- Australia 10, 11, 32, 43, 66, 71, 73, 78, 79, 85, 90, 93, 99, 102, 103, 105, 110, 113, 116
- China 90
- Cyprus 92, 93, 96, 101, 105, 109, 113, 115
- Finland (1000 Lakes) 10, 11, 13, 44, 53, 59, 71, 73, 77, 88, 89, 92, 97, 101, 105, 110, 115
- Germany 101, 105, 110, 113, 115
- Great Britain (RAC) 11, 21, 32, 35, 40, 49, 50, 53, 54, 58, 59, 64-66, 78, 80, 81, 85, 89, 90, 93, 97, 103, 105, 107, 110, 114, 115
- Hong Kong – Beijing 52, 59
- Indonesia 69, 73, 77
- Japan 110, 113, 115, 116
- Malaysia 73
- Mexico 35, 36, 109, 110, 113
- Monte Carlo 30, 33, 44, 48, 55, 60, 62, 63, 75, 76, 83, 88, 90, 91, 96, 101, 103, 109, 113
- New Zealand 10, 11, 38, 52, 56, 58, 62,

65, 77, 85, 89, 92, 93, 97, 98, 102, 103, 108, 109, 115
- Portugal 27, 57, 62, 64, 65, 77, 81, 84, 89, 92, 96
- Safari 9, 10, 22, 28, 48, 52, 68, 71, 76, 77, 84, 89, 91, 92, 96, 97, 101
- San Remo 57, 59, 72, 73, 78, 85, 90, 93, 97, 101, 102, 105
- Sardinia 110
- Spain (Catalunya) 47, 63, 66, 73, 74, 77, 84, 89, 92, 96, 101, 105, 110, 116
- Sweden 10, 11, 48, 61, 64, 67, 71, 75, 77, 81, 84, 88, 91, 96, 101, 103, 104, 109, 112, 113
- Thailand 71
- Tour de Corse (Corsica) 22, 25, 34, 57, 65, 77, 82-84, 89, 93, 97, 101, 105, 106, 110, 113, 115, 116
- Turkey 103, 110, 115
Richards, David 9, 26, 38, 39, 40, 42, 46, 59, 66
Rothmans cigarette sponsorship 9, 38, 39, 59

Sainz, Carlos 10, 73, 76, 77, 84, 90, 101, 105, 106
Seat 87
Stevens, Peter 26, 28, 34
Subaru Tecnica Internationale (STI) 9, 10, 25, 26, 38, 39, 40

Subaru models:
- 360 model 16
- Justy 12
- Legacy family 9, 11, 12, 16, 18-20, 22, 24, 40, 43, 52-54, 58, 59
- Leone 12, 16
- R1 mini-car 12
- Retna model 26
Subaru works drivers and co-drivers:
- Atkinson, Chris 113, 116
- Alen, Markku 10, 52, 53
- Arai, Toshihiro 97
- Bourne, 'Possum' 10, 49, 52, 59, 66
- Burns, Richard 32, 40, 41, 59, 65, 66, 85-93, 95-100, 102
- Eriksson, Kenneth 68, 71, 73, 75-78, 81, 84
- Grist, Nicky 43, 76, 79, 84
- Hirvonen, Mikko 108
- Kankkunen, Juha 15, 30, 31, 86, 88-92
- Liatti, Piero 25, 63, 65, 69, 71, 73, 75-78, 81, 84-86
- Makinen, Tommi 10, 14, 34, 35, 44, 45, 100-105
- Martin, Markko 93, 97, 99
- McRae, Colin 11, 25, 26, 27, 30, 39, 41-44, 46-48, 52, 53-67, 69-73, 75-86, 110
- Mills, Phil 49, 103, 107

- Reid, Robert 40
- Ringer, Derek 39, 43, 56
- Sainz, Carlos 10, 21, 44, 46-48, 54, 55, 57, 59-66
- Sarrazin, Stephene 113
- Solberg, Petter 35, 36, 40, 44, 48-50, 93, 95-97, 100-110, 112-116
- Thiry, Bruno 86, 89
- Vatanen, Ari 11, 38, 39, 52-54

Talbot (and models) 40
Toyota (and models) 9-16, 23, 46, 48, 52, 54, 57, 59, 62, 65, 66, 84, 85, 88, 90
Triumph (and models) 39
Turner, Stuart 11

Vauxhall (and models) 4 2
VW (and models) 17, 18

Wilson, Malcolm 98
World Championship for Makes 40, 42, 54, 58, 60, 66, 71, 74, 80, 84, 91, 100, 103, 108, 109
World Drivers' Championship 38, 39, 41-44, 54, 60, 64, 66, 92, 93, 99, 103, 106, 107, 109
World Rallying 40

ISBN: 978-1-787113-24-4
In nine eventful years – 1957 to 1965 – the six-cylinder-engined Austin Healey evolved into a formidable and increasingly specialised rally car. By any standards, it was the first of the 'homologation specials' – a type made progressively stronger, faster, more versatile, and more suitable for the world's toughest international rallies. This is the story ...

ISBN: 978-1-787113-25-1
Four-wheel-drive was authorised in rallying from 1979, but for a time no serious car manufacturer even tried to harness it to their cars. Peugeot designed, developed, campaigned and won with the first truly sophisticated four-wheel-drive Group B Car – the 205 Turbo 16; the first truly great, purpose-designed Group B car. Determined to win at almost any cost, Peugeot hired Jean Todt in 1981, and set him an ambitious target: his dream car had to be running in 1983, homologated in 1984, and capable of winning World Championships by 1985. Packed with illustrations, technical details, facts, figures and successes of this innovative car, this exciting book is a must for any rally fan.

ISBN 978-1-787111-07-3
This book describes the birth, development, and rallying career of the original Ford Escort, one of Europe's landmark rally cars in the early 1970s, providing a compact and authoritative history of where, how and why it became so important to the sport.

ISBN 978-1-787111-08-0
This book describes the birth, development, and rallying career of the Lancia Stratos, Europe's very first purpose-built rally car, in the mid/late 1970s, providing a compact and authoritative history of where, when and how it became so important to the sport.

ISBN: 978-1-787111-10-3
The Audi Quattro was the world's first successful four-wheel-drive rally car. It brought new standards to the sport, and inspired many others to copy it. This is the complete story.

ISBN: 978-1-787111-11-0
Fiat entered rallying in 1970, with the aim of becoming World Rally Champion – and it was the 131 Abarth of 1976-1980 which made that possible. It soon began winning World rallies, and, in 1977, 1978 and 1980, the 'works' team also won the World Championship for Makes, paving the way for successors the Lancia Rally 037 and the Delta Integrale.

ISBN 978-1-845848-70-5
The inside story of how the giant-killing Minis of rallying, rallycross and racing fame were converted from standard Mini-Coopers in the BMC Competitions Department. The author, who spent 22 years in 'Comps', reveals the secrets of specification, build technique and development of the famous Works Minis. The book includes contributions from Ginger Devlin (Cooper's Chief Mechanic) and 'Jumping Jeff' Williamson (Works Rallycross driver).

ISBN 978-1-787113-30-5
Brian Moylan spent 22 years with the Competition Department preparing cars for international rallies and travelling the world to provide service support. During this period, Big Healeys, Minis and TR7s were amongst the front runners in the world rally scene, though many other BMC/BL models also saw use as rally cars. This is the fascinating tale as seen from a mechanic's point of view how BMC/BL rally cars evolved during this important period.

ISBN 978-1-845849-94-8
The inside story of the legendary BMC Works Competitions Department as told by the three Competition Managers. Based on previously unpublished internal memos and documents, and the recollections of the prime movers, here are the ups and downs, and the politics of big time competition in an exciting era.

ISBN 978-1-787112-29-2
This book covers the pre-WRC golden years, the Rally of the Forest period. With access to crew notes and manufacturers' archives, and containing many previously unpublished pictures, the history and excitement of the RAC International Rally of Great Britain has been captured in *RAC Rally Action!*